Our President's Mission to Asia

Geopolitics Is a Dinosaur! The Future Is a Community of Common Destiny

by Helga Zepp-LaRouche

Zepp-LaRouche leads the German political party, Civil Rights Movement Solidarity (BüSo).

Oct. 28—There is some very good news: The presidents of the three most important nuclear powers in the world are working intensively to improve relations among their countries and put them on a solid foundation of cooperation in their mutual interest. One might think that these developments would be enthusiastically commented upon in Europe, since they mean that the danger of a major war—one that could possibly exterminate all mankind—may thereby be averted. But far from it! Instead, these days the three presidents have one thing in common: They are equally maligned by the mainstream media—although with different predicates—as terrifying bogeymen, various called mentally unstable, a new Stalin, a dictator. This distorted view comes from wearing geopolitical glasses.

Less than two weeks before his trip to Asia—when he will visit Japan, South Korea, the Philippines, and Vietnam, and make a two-day state visit to China—President Trump stressed, in an interview with Lou Dobbs on the Fox News television channel, that it would be great if the United States had a good relationship with the nuclear power Russia, and that this would make a solution to the North Korean crisis much easier. Trump, who was supposed to have been intimidated by the intelligence community's concocted fable of "Russia-gate" on precisely this issue, stressed: "If we had a [good] relationship with Russia, that would be a good thing, not a bad thing."

Trump also reported that he had telephoned President Xi Jinping and congratulated him on his re-election as General Secretary of the Chinese Communist Party: "He's a powerful man. I happen to think he's a very good person. Now with that being said, he represents China, I represent the USA, so, you know, there's going to always be conflict. But we have a very good relationship. People say we have the best relationship of any president-president, because he's called president also." Trump added that he hoped his upcoming trip to Asia would be historic and very positive.

The Chinese Party Congress

There is legitimate hope for such a result in light of the new era, which was been further consolidated by China at the just concluded 19th Congress of the Chinese Communist Party. For, largely ignored or misunderstood by western commentators, President Xi Jinping, in the various aspects of his foreign policy in particular, has laid the groundwork for a new model of international relations, , one of "the community of a shared future for mankind," and China is ready to take global responsibility for its success.

This concept has been ignored in the western media; instead, these media have chosen to focus on the fact that Xi designated no apparent successor, although that was of minor importance given his re-election for a five-year term.

One is reminded of the valet whom Hegel mentions in his *Phenomenology of Mind*, who only sees the underwear of the world-historical individual he serves, but never the ideas that inspire his master. Obviously the people in the media simply assign the concept of "the community of a common destiny" to the category of propaganda, as they would the usual language with which western parties stress their commitment to "democracy, a free market economy, and human rights"—it belongs to the party litany, but is really only empty phrases.

But this is not the case for Xi Jinping and the Chinese Communist Party, which has put itself fully and totally behind Xi Jinping's philosophy of this global commu-

EDITORIAL

nity of common destiny. The real objective of the New Silk Road policy is precisely to create a higher level of reason wherein mutually beneficial economic cooperation, "win-win cooperation," overcomes geopolitics, and puts the interests of mankind as a whole before the interests of any single nation or alliance of nations.

Over recent years, Xi Jinping has often addressed the "old, obsolete model" of the West, which looks at the world geopolitically with a Cold War mentality and as a zero-sum game, and that theme has been debated by many Chinese scholars. To this, Xi has counterposed an entirely new concept, the idea of a community of common destiny for mankind.

Seen from this vantage point, there is indeed a perspective from which all the problems of this earth can be solved from a higher level. In this way we can overcome the backward, imperial outlook of Winston Churchill—that the Empire can have neither permanent friends or enemies, only permanent interests—and the limited conviction in this respect of Charles de Gaulle (despite all sympathy with him as an individual)—that nations have no friends, only interests.

In contrast, the idea of a community with a shared future for mankind corresponds to the thinking of Nicholas of Cusa, expressed in his Coincidence of Opposites (*Coincidentia Oppositorum*). His idea is that man can think on a higher level of reason, on which the contradictions found on the lower level of understanding can be overcome; in other words, the One possesses a higher power than the Many. From the standpoint of universal history, it is obvious that the attainment of the common aims of mankind will determine the era in which humankind will grow up, so to speak, and demonstrate its true character as a creative species.

Progress Is Underway

Thanks to the arrogance of western politicians and the media, it has generally gone unnoticed that Xi Jinping's conception of a community of shared future for mankind was adopted as an official resolution on March 23 of this year by the 34th Session of the UN Human Rights Commission, and thus in a sense incorporated into international law.

While most countries in Asia are engaged in the Silk Road dynamic, and are undergoing strategic realignments from this perspective—such as Japan's rapprochement with Russia and China—the western media have commented on this development through the distorted optics previously mentioned. For example, Japanese Foreign Minister Taro Kono said, in an interview with the daily *Nikkei* newspaper, that, on the occasion of President Trump's forthcoming visit, he would like to initiate a dialogue among Japan, the United States, India, and Australia on the highest level, to improve cooperation on questions of free trade and security in the entire region from the South China Sea, to the Indian Ocean, to Africa. *Deutsche Welle*, Germany's public international broadcaster, interprets that as being an alternative to China's Belt and Road policy.

But what did Indian Foreign Secretary Subrahmanyam Jaishankar say about it to *Sputnik?* "I do not think projecting our cooperation as competition with China does justice to our side. . . . It's important that India-Japan relations not be defined in negative terms. Every movie doesn't require a villain. Asia, particularly South Asia, is so under-connected, that any connectivity which comes in is good for this, provided it follows broad principles, is sustainable, and is respectful of local sensitivity." *Sputnik* reported that Japan wants to invest $110 billion in Asian nations over the next five years, and that India is participating in connectivity projects in Myanmar and Bangladesh, and wants to develop the Andaman and Nicobar islands in cooperation with Japan. Jaishankar stressed that, due to the enormous infrastructure deficit, it makes sense to work together, instead of undercutting each other.

For geopolitically oriented commentators, the main thing is that the South Asians should not talk about the "Belt and Road Initiative" associated with China, but rather about building "connectivity." In practical terms, what is important for the people in the region is that they are finally getting loans for infrastructure investments—previously denied them by the IMF and World Bank—through new financial institutions such as the Asian Infrastructure Investment Bank, New Development Fund, New Silk Road Fund, SAARC Development Fund, and similar institutions—all heavily funded by China.

Beyond that, the program outlined in the *EIR* report titled, *The New Silk Road Becomes the World Land-Bridge*, envisions a Land-Bridge that connects all continents through infrastructure and provides the landlocked regions with the same advantages that previously redounded only to regions on oceans and rivers.

The good news is that the majority of mankind is moving into a new, more beautiful era; the bad news is that most European politicians and media remain stuck in the old, obsolete thinking and are falling further behind the curve of developments.

But, as the motto of our newspaper says, *"The age of Schiller is coming!"*

EIR Contents

www.larouchepub.com Volume 44, Number 44, November 3, 2017

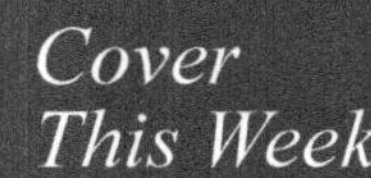

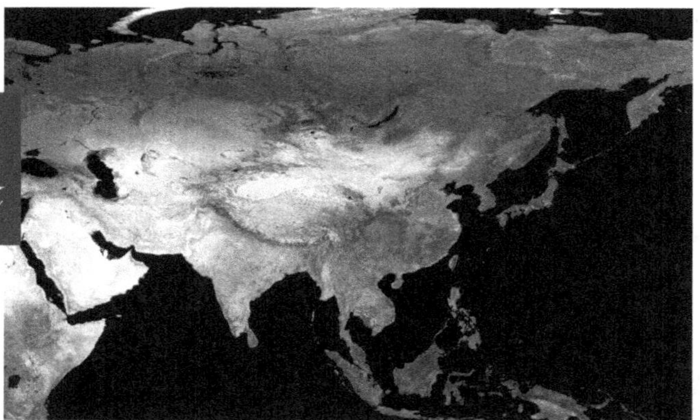

NASA/QSFC

A satellite image of Asia.

OUR PRESIDENT'S MISSION TO ASIA

What's Really Happening in China And What It Means for Americans

This is an edited transcript of the weekly Schiller Institute New Paradigm webcast of Oct. 26 with Helga Zepp-LaRouche.

Harley Schlanger: Hello, I'm Harley Schlanger from the Schiller Institute. Welcome to this week's webcast with Helga Zepp-LaRouche, the founder of the Schiller Institute and its chairwoman.

There have been incredible developments over the last week, starting with the continuation and conclusion of the 19th National Congress of the Communist Party of China (CPC), which laid out an absolutely bold strategic perspective for the next 35 years. This has gotten *very* little coverage in the West, but it's an event which will shape what happens not just in China, but globally. We're going to put that on top of our list for discussion today, but we'll also take up some developments around "Russia-gate" and a few questions that were sent to me during the week.

So, Helga, to start with, the 19th Party Congress which just concluded, really was quite incredible, putting forward the idea of a "beautiful China" creating a "beautiful world." What's your impression?

Helga Zepp-LaRouche: First of all, I would like to note the fact that the Western media, in their non-coverage and what they decide to focus on, are just completely ridiculous. Their main attention was directed to the fact that Xi Jinping did not present a visible successor. He was just voted in for five more years. This is obviously not the key point.

Xinhua/Ju Peng

Xi Jinping, President of China and General Secretary of the China Communist Party, greeting participants at the 19th CPC National Congress in Beijing, Oct. 25, 2017.

What this Congress represents is a strategic shift. It is in line with the Belt and Road Initiative and the new model of international relations China has developed under the leadership of President Xi Jinping, and I think the West has not caught up with what this is actually all about. They are so much behind the curve, it is almost absurd.

What Xi Jinping has accomplished in the five years of his Presidency so far, the previous five years, is that he has successfully taken on some of the problems China had, such as corruption, such as a slowing economy, and various other problems, and he has actually been extremely successful.

Everybody who has been in China and has looked at China without prejudices, could not help but notice it— that it has led to a population which for the most part is very satisfied—83% of the people are absolutely happy

Street scene in Shanghai, April 2, 2011.

about what the government is doing. I would like to see the Western country that has such approval ratings.

But what has happened at this 19th Party Congress is truly amazing. In a little more more than a week Xi Jinping has consolidated the party around a manifold perspective, of which I want to start to discuss various aspects:

First of all, in the immediate next three years, by 2020, the aim is to eliminate poverty, to lift the remaining 42 million people who are presently living in poverty in China, above that level. Now, that compares with a similar number of people currently living in poverty in the United States, except that China has about four times the population of the United States, and it compares with the roughly 120 million poor people in the European Union (EU), who have been poor for the last 20 years, with nothing being done about it; there's no perspective to eliminate poverty in the EU.

From 2020 to 2035, the aim is to make China a moderately prosperous, functioning socialist country; and then from 2035 to 2050, China is to become a completely developed, culturally harmonious, advanced, democratic, socialist and beautiful country.

There is an additional element. First of all, what impressed me very much is the focus of Xi Jinping, and also other people who spoke, on the purpose of all this—namely, that it is the improvement of the life of people, that people should live a better life, a happier life. That is completely lacking in the discussion in the West: That the aim of politics is that people should be happy! The pursuit of Happiness is an inalienable right,

which was after all in the Declaration of Independence of the young United States.

But there is another aspect to it. Xi Jinping, especially in his concluding remarks, spoke about a socialist model with Chinese characteristics for a new era. And the aim which was formulated very explicitly, was that China will take a global role in creating a beautiful future for all of mankind. Now, that is really something! When has any Western politician had a vision of creating a beautiful future for all of humanity? You have to go back a long way, until you find people even thinking in these terms. China has provided a model of international governance and international relationships based on the sovereignty and respect for the social model of the other country, non-interference, with no attempt to change the system to the Western model or to their own model, but to respect the other countries' sovereignty.

This is an incredible perspective, because if you look at it from the long arc of human history, this was an initiative which *had* to be made at a certain point in the development of humanity. There *had* to be at some point, somebody to say, "we are the human species, the human species is one"—Xi Jinping always calls it the "shared community for the future of mankind"—somebody to put forth a vision of how we can organize our affairs on this planet in such a way that the result is a good life for all people living on this planet.

Westerners tend to not understand that. They tend to either overlook it or denounce it as propaganda, just communist rhetoric; or they cannot imagine that it could be true, because they themselves are so unused to thinking in these terms. The poor power of their imagination is completely unable to imagine that there could be a political leader who thinks that way. But I'm absolutely convinced that Xi Jinping *is* a Confucian man, that he wants to shape the world in a Confucian harmonic way. People in the West who want to understand what's going on, should not just push it aside, but really try to grasp it. Because it's a tremendous potentiality for all of humanity, which must be supported and should be taken up. And I think it's important that people

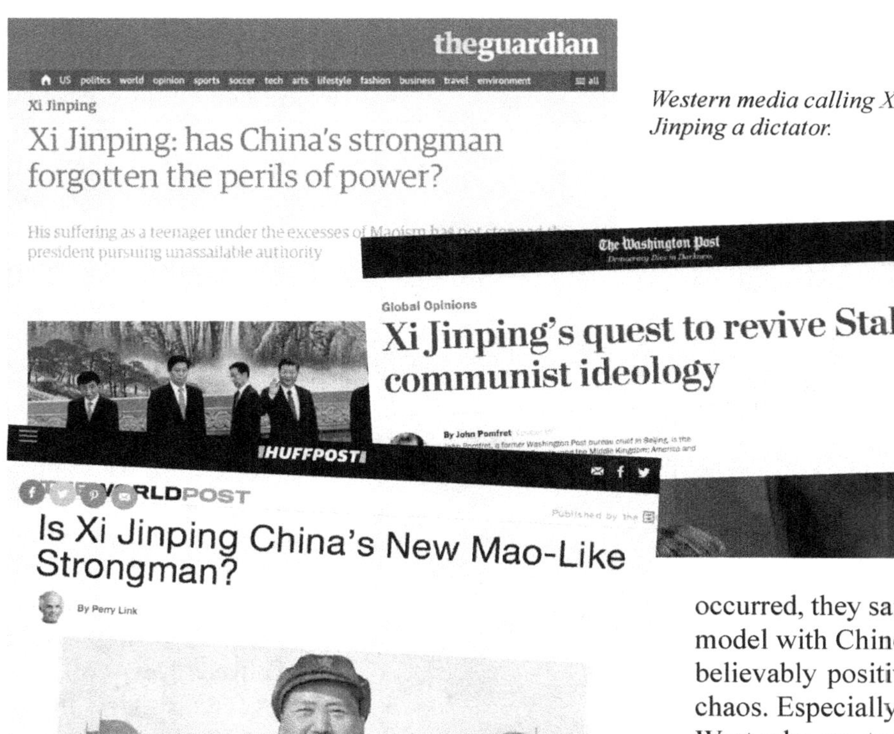

Western media calling Xi Jinping a dictator.

achieve the intellectual integrity to try to comprehend what he is talking about.

Schlanger: I found it very interesting that Xi traced the period that he described as a "miserable period for China," to the Opium War, the British Empire's efforts to force the Chinese to accept opium shipped into China by the British. Because that makes it clear that he's talking about China emerging from under an imperial system into a new era.

Zepp-LaRouche: Yes. Also very noticeable is that, preceding and during this party congress, the attacks by the Western media against China were just unbelievable, blaming China for the coming crash, and decrying the debt of China—while, in reality, every debt China has incurred is covered by capital assets, because they have invested in the real economy and infrastructure, and therefore in assets which would be there if there were a crash—unlike the Western investments in speculation, in derivatives, which are just virtual and will disappear the moment the crash occurs.

There was an unbelievable barrage of attacks also against President Xi Jinping himself—totally insane comparisons to all kinds of historical figures; it was just

absolutely berserk. I noticed a new tone of self-confidence in the way the Chinese media responded to these attacks. They very self-assuredly said that the West does not get it, they don't understand China, they don't try to understand China; but moreover, the Chinese model is so clearly superior to the Western model.

In the past, the Chinese have been much more restrained and have held back from saying such things—but now, when these attacks occurred, they said: But look at it, the Chinese socialist model with Chinese characteristics is having these unbelievably positive results, while in the West there is chaos. Especially if you look at the EU, or those in the West who are trying to export their model of Western democracy and human rights. And then they say, those people in the West who speak like that, obviously don't want China to succeed, and they think China is only doing well when it submits to Western values—but when China is developing, then they regard China as a threat to their world order.

That is just completely ridiculous, they say, and therefore, since the West is collapsing and the influence of the Western media is vanishing, one can just ignore what these Western media are saying.

That is a new tone, and I really like that. There was just a poll in the United States which found that 57% of Americans—more than half—do not believe a word of what is said in the mainstream media. This is quite significant. Obviously the influence of these media is shrinking; they have overdone it; they have tried to pretend that they control everything, including the way people should interpret democratic elections in the United States. But they have overblown it, and I think there is a blowback, and I think that that creates a very interesting new situation.

As for China, everybody should study the speeches of Xi Jinping. There is also a very interesting new three-part documentary on CGTN TV about Xi Jinping, which those who want to understand the man should just watch [*China: The Time of Xi*]. But study his speeches. When I did so over the years, I was very im-

High-speed train in China.

pressed by the fact that he always puts a lot of emphasis on traditional Chinese culture; he also knows the best periods of the cultures of other countries. When he travels, he always emphasizes the best contributions of the other culture, which I think is very important. He also puts a lot of emphasis on beauty, on the spirit of science. He's a Renaissance man! We have not been used to having Renaissance men for a long time. My husband is one of them, but they are a rare species. I think people have a lot to discover if they engage in becoming familiar with Xi Jinping.

Schlanger: I found one other thing quite significant, which is, in contrast to the nonsense in the media about Xi personally and about the direction of China, President Trump, when he called Xi Jinping right after the congress ended, congratulated him and spoke of his "elevation," that is, his re-election, in positive terms.

The President is heading to Asia soon. Can you update us on the prospects for that trip?

Zepp-LaRouche: President Trump will be accompanied by a very large delegation of American businessmen. I am pretty sure that what will be discussed, both in Japan and also in China, is large Japanese-Chinese investments in American infrastructure. Those who are familiar with the activities of the Schiller Institute, probably know that we have campaigned in the

United States since 2014 for the idea that the United States should fully cooperate with the New Silk Road, with the Belt and Road Initiative—and I think this will be on the agenda. I'm pretty sure that the Chinese government and Xi Jinping, especially now with the accomplishment of the 19th Party Congress, will not miss the opportunity to offer something to Trump, who is obviously in a very difficult situation. American infrastructure is in terrible condition; the United States has only 150 km of high-speed rail, between New York and Boston, compared with far more than 20,000 km network of high-speed rail in China. China will have all its major cities connected by high-speed rail by 2020, just three years from now, and then they will have a 50,000 km network of high-speed rail.

The Schiller Institute has proposed for some time now, that the United States needs a similar high-speed rail system connecting its East Coast, its West Coast, and maybe even build some new cities in the middle of the United States. The United States could have something like 50,000 km (35,000 miles) of high-speed rail. I think that's one area of cooperation, in investment in infrastructure. On the other hand, American businessmen and American firms could and should be investing in the many, many projects of the Belt and Road Initiative in Asia, Latin America, and Africa. A completely new level of international cooperation is on the horizon.

I cannot predict for sure whether this will happen, but it's obviously a direct potentiality. Should this occur, given that President Trump is very inclined to improve relations with Russia, which he reiterated in a recent interview, and if the three countries, the United States, China and Russia can find a way of cooperating, I'm absolutely optimistic that this would represent a new era of civilization. Should President Trump move in this direction—I've said many times, sticking my neck out and putting my reputation on the line—then

President Trump has the potential to become one of the greatest Presidents in the history of the United States.

Many people will be absolutely shocked at my saying that, but anybody who is not a complete moron should be happy if the three largest nuclear powers reach understanding and cooperation. With the "win-win" offer, the new era offered by China, the possibility to overcome geopolitics forever is clearly there.

Most people have no inkling, no idea that that potentiality of a completely new era of civilization is before us. I simply ask all our viewers to not just believe me— that's not the point—but to investigate it for themselves. Because this is one of, in German we say, the *"Sternstunden der Menschheit"*— one of those star-hours of humanity, or decisive moments for humanity. In a sense this moment is different, it has an incredible promise similar to the fall of the Berlin Wall. That was one such star-hour of humanity, which as we now know, retrospectively, was missed, because geopolitics marched in: George Bush, Sr., Margaret Thatcher, and François Mitterrand—were all determined to prevent this opportunity for mankind from leading to a new era.

This time, however, we are on the verge, on the eve, or maybe in the morning at sunrise of such a new era, in a much more powerful way, because it's already a reality for about 100 nations. So people must really understand, this is a *punctum saliens*, as Friedrich Schiller would call it, where the entire direction of the human drama of history could go into a completely new stage and a new direction. We are very close to that. The only thing lacking is the West's grasping it and joining it.

Schlanger: It's not a coincidence that the same media that are attacking President Xi and attacking the Chinese model, are behind Russia-gate. Their continued efforts to come up with some smoking gun, to try to get rid of Trump—there's a whole new series of articles about the 25th Amendment—but something that happened in this last week, which is in part a result of the

Bundesregierung/Kugler

President Donald Trump (center) in conversation with Russian President Vladimir Putin (right) at the July 7, 2017 G-20 Summit. European Commission President Jean-Claude Juncker is on the left.

work that we've done, getting out the Mueller dossier, but also the work by some of the Republicans in Congress, to go after the authors of the "sex dossier" against Trump. As you know, Helga, it came out that Hillary Clinton's campaign and the Democratic National Committee funded that Fusion GPS/Christopher Steele sex memo.

This obviously turns things upside down, doesn't it?

Zepp-LaRouche: Well, it was sort of to be suspected that that was the case, but now it's out and I think there's a lot of egg on the faces of Hillary Clinton and the whole Democratic National Committee (DNC), because they lied, and they knew they were lying. They used foreign [British] intelligence against their own elected President.

I think there will be a big aftermath, and I think the timing is very good that this story is coming out now, because it brings the entire Russia-gate narrative to its final end, which process was started with the Veteran Intelligence Professionals for Sanity (VIPS) memo of July 24. It frees up President Trump for his upcoming Asia trip.

Another point which I think is worthwhile to reflect on, is that all the Europeans believed this Russian electoral interference story, and went with it as 100% true, and are also saying now, that this is proof that Russia will manipulate European elections and internal affairs. But I think people should reflect on this whole thing,

Ex-FBI director Robert Mueller is heading a task force to investigate the Trump Administration.

and really understand what the British empire is, what this apparatus is—it's called "deep state" by some, but I think it's really, fundamentally, the old paradigm of geopolitical thinking, of the Western financial system which goes for high profit, and which defends the interest of its privileged class—in total contrast to the new system, the new model, the new paradigm, which aims at the common good of the people, and a better, happier life for everybody on this planet.

So it's really the fight between these two systems: It's terrible, I almost feel pity for the Clintons, because they really look terribly bad now. But I think it's very good for history that the truth has come out, and it will give a lot of impetus to this trip of President Trump.

Schlanger: And it also gives President Trump a certain amount of credibility that the media have been trying to take away from him, because he's been insisting from the beginning that there's no story here, and it's a fraudulent attempt to undercut him.

I got an email from someone who asked if you could talk about the significance of the Catalan separatist movement, in the context of this fight between the old paradigm and the new; I think there's been a lot of confusion about what it represents, partly coming from the European Union itself.

So, what's behind this, and why is it happening?

Zepp-LaRouche: The Catalonia development is also an effect of the neo-con/neo-liberal paradigm. In Spain, as in Greece, Italy, and Portugal, the populations were hit by the absolutely brutal austerity of the Troika. Despite the fact that many young people and many skilled laborers have left, Spain still has an unemployment rate among the youth of, I think, up to 60%—young people who neither have a job, nor are in education, which means they have no future!

This is something which has hit all of Spain, and an Italian Member of the European Parliament named Marco Zanni said correctly, that the fight between the Catalans and the Spanish federal government is a fight between the poor and the poorer. I think that that is what triggered the unwillingness of the Catalans to continue to pay the federal government—so the trigger, therefore, is in the overall policy of the Troika. Like the Brexit, or the victory of President Trump, or the "no" to the referendum in Italy, or the recent election result in Austria, or the Czech Republic—all of these reflect the discontent of the people with the neo-liberal economic policy.

But there are other features. Of course it is wrong for the Catalans to demand independence, because it goes against Spain's constitution, and we cannot have a "Europe of the regions," because this is the design, not only of the federalist movement of Coudenhove-Kalergi, of the Pan-European Union, but of the British who are supporting the Catalans openly in all their newspapers, because they want the destruction of the nation-state. If you have 50 or 100 small regional entities all being "independent," as compared to the supra-national institution of the EU, they would have absolutely no power, and therefore the common good of the people could not be defended. The significance of the emergence of the nation-state was that it is the only institution which, especially in times of crisis, defends the common good of the people, not the private interests. So there is that aspect of it.

But then there is also another point, which I think President Putin of Russia pointed to. He said: Well, the West was so emphatic in pushing democracy, democracy, democracy, and they developed this double standard. Democracy and independence for Kosovo is fine, but of course, now they are caught in a paradox, because if the same thing happens to a pro-EU government like that of Prime Minister Rajoy [of Spain], then of course there is a contradiction, because there is no good solution. If the Catalans declare indepen-

Catalan demonstrators in Barcelona seeking independence from Spain, Oct. 3, 2017.

cc/Sasha Popovic

dence, and Rajoy allows it, that threatens the integrity of the Spanish state, so he cannot do that. On the other hand, if he tries to quell the masses in the streets by the use of military means or police power—there were hundreds of thousands of people in the streets in Barcelona and there will probably be as many again in these coming days—then that is terrible for all the values the EU is supposed to represent, such as democracy and human rights, and other things in that category of issues.

So it's a paradox. There is no solution within that system.

We have said, very clearly, the *only* way you can remedy this situation is for Spain to fully become a hub in the New Silk Road, which Rajoy already wants Spain to do. Only when the Iberian peninsula is fully developed as part of the Belt and Road Initiative, can the tensions between the different provinces of Spain be overcome. By the way, the leader of the Basque region has also already come out in support for the Catalans, so this has a tremendously explosive potential.

There is one other aspect to add and that is that in Spain, a dossier came out which we have not yet been fully able to look into, but it mentions that the Catalan independence movement is supported by George Soros, by the Ukrainian Maidan forces, and by [Gene] Sharp, who is the author of the whole "color revolution" program cooked up in Oxford and Cambridge. So this is a big story, and we will investigate and look into it further. Because Soros is the main force behind a lot of these color revolutions, including that in the United States.

The right answer is clearly the Belt and Road Initiative, the New Silk Road, common development for all—and then a solution can be found. In that light, I think it's very positive that Wang Yi, the Chinese foreign minister, just met with his Ukrainian counterpart [Pavlo Klimkin], and Ukraine and China said that they want to cooperate very closely in the Belt and Road Initiative. Here again, what we have said for years, the only way that you can solve the Ukraine crisis—where the west of Ukraine is Western oriented, Catholic, and the eastern part, is Orthodox, Russian oriented—the only way to get back to the unity of Ukraine, is if the Eurasian Land-Bridge, the New Silk Road, is in construction from the Atlantic to the Pacific. In that way, a higher level of cooperation is implemented, which then solves all of these conflicts. So that is also a very promising development.

Schlanger: As your husband always says, "when you're confronted with two bad choices, always choose the third." And that's what we see with Spain and with the Belt and Road Initiative overall.

Helga, next week, when we convene for the webcast, we'll be on the eve of Trump's visit to Asia, in particular his meeting with Xi Jinping [in Beijing]. Any last words of advice for President Trump?

Zepp-LaRouche: Well, I'm optimistic. President Trump is a good businessman. He's becoming a good President, and therefore, he will absolutely recognize the incredible potential, not only for American business interests, but for the United States to become great by being part of a greater whole.

Schlanger: OK, with that, we'll say good-bye, and we'll see you next week.

Zepp-LaRouche: Good-bye.

Party Congress Reaffirms China's Commitment to New Type of Development

by William Jones

Oct. 31—The dramatic changes initiated at the 19th Party Congress of the Chinese Communist Party, which concluded on Oct. 23, are slated to produce deep-going and long-lasting shifts in the party's thought and practice. The incorporation in the Party Constitution of Xi Jinping's concept of "Socialism with Chinese Characteristics for a New Era" marks a significant new direction for China and the world.

One could well mark the shift already in September 2013, when President Xi launched what became known as the Belt and Road Initiative (BRI), one of the most ambitious engineering projects ever attempted. Prior to that, China had pursued the policy laid out in Deng Xiaoping's concept of "reform and opening up" in 1978. Coming out of the devastating period of the disastrous Great Leap Forward (1958-62) and the subsequent Great Proletarian Cultural Revolution (1966-75), the "reform and opening up" marked the entry of China into the world market and an end to the isolation of China that characterized the Cold War period (1947-91).

While China was then entering an economic system that was seriously flawed, and was entering it as a cheap-labor producer, Deng intended to utilize that opening in order to gradually bring China up, technologically and economically, to a significantly higher level. The success of that policy over the last 40 years has been breathtaking in its scope.

At the same time, Deng's policy focused on having China maintain a low political profile on the international stage, while slowly building up its economic capacity and raising its people to a decent standard of living. But it was clear that if the policy were successful, as even Napoleon had foreseen two centuries ago, China, with a population of well over a billion people, would be playing a major role on the international scene, not only economically but also politically. The Belt and Road Initiative (BRI) was the debut of modern China's entry onto the world stage as a shaper of global policy.

But it would be a mistake to view this shift in terms of traditional geopolitics, as the "fake news" media has portrayed it: Xi was trying to "grab power," to bring in

his "cronies" into the top leadership, and to change the rules of the game to secure his position.

Look at the seven members of the new Standing Committee, the highest policy-making body in the party: only two had worked closely with Xi earlier, while the others had no particular relationship to him. It was obviously something else which had caused them to merit promotion. The fake news media also harped on the idea that Xi would break with the rules and keep close his old collaborator on the old Standing Committee, Wang Qishan, who had reached the mandatory age of retirement. Much to the chagrin of the China-bashers, Wang Qishan retired in good order from the Standing Committee.

Nor is China inclined to become the leading "hegemon" in a fragile and failing system—but rather, it seeks to change this flawed system into one which not only works, but works for the benefit of all peoples. For this reason, the colossal infrastructure project that is the Belt and Road Initiative has won the overwhelming support of the world's people, particularly in the developing sector, which has the most to benefit from the BRI's shift toward infrastructural investment.

Since the early fight in the 1970s over the Third World's demand for a New World Economic Order and the creation of an International Development Bank—a 1975 proposal by economist Lyndon LaRouche which at the time won wide adherence from developing sector countries—the post-Bretton Woods system has offered little to these countries except more poverty and misery.

The BRI and the creation of the Asian Infrastructure Investment Bank (AIIB)—founded in December 2015 —were a clarion call to these nations, announcing that real development was once more on the table. Since then, China has been one of the most active countries in reshaping foreign policy in many parts of the globe. President Xi's call for replacing the zero-sum game of geopolitics with a win-win "community for a shared future for mankind" has also won great support among many countries of the world, even among the developed countries. Helga Zepp-LaRouche has characterized it as a new Peace of Westphalia, comparing it to the peace that ended Europe's brutal Thirty Years' War in 1648 with the notion of working for "the good of the other."

Major Changes

The 19th Party Congress accomplished this shift, including the Belt and Road Initiative, which has now been incorporated into the party constitution. It has become the *leitmotif* of all party activity. As this does reflect a shift from the low-profile early years of "reform and opening up" beginning in 1978, there is, no doubt, some apprehension among many party members about the shift. Not only does it place a greater responsibility on China to see to it that the Belt and Road succeeds, but it also puts China more in the spotlight, which can have negative effects whenever obstacles are met along the road.

Already now, there are projects in the works to study the implications of this "new era" policy. Beijing's Renmin University is setting up an entire department to study "Socialism with Chinese Characteristics for a New Era." At the heart of the policy, as President Xi underlined in his Work Report, is the whole-hearted commitment of the Chinese Communist Party and its members to improve the conditions of life of the Chinese people, a policy which restores and reinvigorates the role of the party in the life of the common man.

Immediately following the Congress, an additional post-Congress press conference was held to elucidate some of the main ideas presented in President Xi's Congress Work Report, initiating a discussion which will be continuing in the weeks and months ahead.

And in an important gesture, filled with symbolism, President Xi traveled, with the other members of the newly elected Standing Committee, to Jiaxing in east China's Zhejiang province, the site where the first CPC National Congress was held in 1921. Each Standing Committee member reaffirmed the oath taken by all members when they join the Communist Party. And while the 19th Party Congress may well be compared to the captain of the ship of state bringing together his officers and crew to re-establish clear guidelines and a compass to indicate the direction the ship is to take on on this new voyage of exploration, at the same time, President Xi was also intent on reassuring the world community that China's rise as a world power would mean closer collaboration and partnership with other countries, both big and small.

In his Work Report, Xi was very clear on this point: "We [nations of the world] should stick together through thick and thin," he said, "to promote trade and investment, liberalization and facilitation, and make economic globalization more open, inclusive, and balanced, so that the benefits are shared by all. We should respect the diversity of civilizations. Let us replace estrangements with exchange, clashes with mutual learning, and superiority with co-existence."

"China will actively promote international cooperation through the Belt and Road Initiative," Xi continued. "In doing so, we hope to achieve policy, infrastructure, trade, financial and people-to-people connectivity, and thus build a new platform for international cooperation to create new drivers of shared development."

Xi recognizes that no country is more important to establish cooperation with than the United States. Speaking to visiting U.S. scholars and businessmen after the Congress, Xi told them: "China is willing to work with the U.S. side to look far ahead and aim high, take each other's interests and concerns into consideration, properly solve differences, and jointly promote China-U.S. cooperation so as to realize a mutually beneficial and win-win situation. We are optimistic about the prospects for China-U.S. relations."

Some have called this new policy "globalization with Chinese characteristics." And yet, while the policy bears something of a Confucian character, it also appeals to a more universal ideal of global cooperation which transcends any one culture and envelops them all. If President Xi is successful in convincing the other world leaders of the wisdom of this policy, the 19th CPC Party Congress will not only have been a clarion call for the "rejuvenation of the Chinese nation," but a significant catalyst for putting mankind back on the road of technological progress and mutual respect for the disparate variety of cultures that make up our world.

Creativity Unleashed: The Time of Xi

by Michael J. Carr

Oct. 30—Imagine the combined impact of the European Renaissance, the Industrial Revolution, the Marshall Plan, and the Apollo Program. Now multiply that by a thousand and you begin to get an idea of the magnitude of the global change initiated by China's President, Xi Jinping. The developing political, economic, scientific, and cultural transformations are already nothing like mankind has ever experienced.

China: Time of Xi, a documentary released on October 14-16 in three linked episodes, gives just a hint of the astounding developments underway in China. The video, by Meridian Line Films for Discovery Asia and CCTV-English, is available at these links:
  • Episode 1: People's Republic
  • Episode 2: Running China Now
  • Episode 3: All Aboard

Yes, the more people you have, the more problem-solvers you potentially have. In fact, over time it may become possible to super-saturate problems with an abundance of solutions.

In one sense, what President Xi and his people are doing in China is entirely natural. It is the "pursuit of happiness." Xi calls it the "Chinese Dream"—a new concept in Chinese history and philosophy. But it is an *inclusive* idea. He conceives of the Chinese Dream, the American Dream, the African Dream, and so on, harmonizing in a Confucian manner into "the Dream for a Beautiful Future for All Mankind." Shortly after assuming the role of President of China, Xi Jinping announced in 2013 the adoption of a set of ideas and proposals powerfully reflecting those long-since designed and advocated by Lyndon and Helga LaRouche. It is now known as the Belt and Road Initiative (BRI). Xi's action is the final flanking action in a centuries-long process of mankind freeing itself from the imperial financial system currently centered in London and its appendages on Wall Street (and with tentacles in "intelligence agencies," various forms of media, and "educational" institutions).

There is a long history of American and American-allied groupings behind measures taken to promote the development of strong, independent sovereign nations in the Americas, Asia, and Africa, which could become allies against the depredations of the predatory British Imperial political and economic system. (See Anton Chaitkin, "The 'Land-Bridge,' Henry Carey's Global Development Program," in *EIR*, May 2, 1997, and many other articles on the subject in the *EIR* archives.)

Now, imperialism is being overtaken by what John Quincy Adams called a community of sovereign republics. Xi refers to the "community of common destiny."

The BRI is unprecedented in many respects. China has never before stepped out onto the world stage to take a leading role in world affairs. However, now China is strong enough physically, and confident enough in its demonstrated economic methods, to offer to share its proven, successful methods with the entire world.

Books will be written about these historic ideas and events, but we shall begin here with a few observations which can help to overcome the suicidal (British Imperial) influences operating in the West, to bring the whole world together into the Community of Common Destiny of which Xi speaks.

In this video series, Xi is described as "pragmatic." A better description would be "humble, yet independent and audacious." On the one hand, Xi and the leadership of China have humbly listened to advice and criticism from all quarters (of most relevance here, the 40-year dialogue with Lyndon and Helga LaRouche)—yet steadfastly refused to allow the entry of ideas into China which would foster artificial internal division and conflict.

Lyndon LaRouche has always insisted that developing countries must leapfrog into the future using the most cutting-edge infrastructure and technologies. Modern China is audaciously leapfrogging in sector after sector of the economy, moving away from technologies associated with "cheap labor" production methods, to cutting-edge, capital-intensive production methods. The rise in overall productivity provides the basis for reaching the seemingly impossible goal of completely eliminating poverty in China by 2020! But that is only a small step towards Xi's goal of eliminating poverty in the world!

While LaRouche's Four Laws are operating in China now, and spreading steadily around the world, Xi has added further ingredients within China. He not only looks from the top down, but from the bottom up. He has assigned to individual officials personal responsibility for each to work with small groups of 150-200

President Xi's concept, "the Chinese Dream," orients the nation.

families, to come up with the plans for each family to escape poverty.

He not only pursues big dreams on the national and international scales, such as the Belt and Road Initiative, bullet trains, exploration and development of space, fusion power, water projects, and new industries—but also pushes the poor individual to dream, and then work to make that dream reality.

Just because you have been poor for 60 years, that is no reason for you to remain in that condition. What are your interests? capabilities? hobbies? dreams? Do you need access to markets? The Chinese government will work to get the roads, rails, and Internet connections built. Do you need machinery, land, or tools to make your dream come true? If there is any degree of success conceivable in your new plan, we will arrange credits or grants.

With the right infrastructure, the rural producer can sell his or her output via the Internet to the city-dweller, or even create a tourist attraction in the countryside for the skyscraper-dwellers in the city to visit. The human mind is the primary asset—not a useless being eating out the substance of the state!

To cherish and stimulate the activity of the human mind, by multiplying the objects of enterprise, is not among the least considerable of the expedients, by which the wealth of a nation may be promoted.

So said Alexander Hamilton in his *Report on the Subject of Manufactures* in 1791.

Alexander Hamilton is alive and well in China. Xi and his team recognize that the source of wealth lies in the powers of the human mind. Xi takes the term "People's Republic" seriously. Not only is the Republic responsible for the welfare of the People, but it recognizes the People as its primary asset, the source of its current power and future potentials.

Renaissance Man

As Helga Zepp-LaRouche recently said, Xi is a modern-day Renaissance man. You may recall that Nicholas of Cusa in many respects laid the basis of the European Renaissance with his concept of the "coincidence of opposites." It is a method of approaching problems that seeks to find a unity, or superseding principle, between or above two or more apparent opposites. He used this approach in solving many problems, and thereby overthrew the dominance in Europe of the Aristotelian approach to the world.

In the Aristotelian view, science and philosophy are just tools of social control: "We already know everything we need to know via sense perception. Don't ask outlandish questions. Shut up and do as you are told! If you are poor or afflicted, it is because you were born that way or so destined. End of story."

Even though Cusa overthrew Aristotle long ago, the

British empire and its appendages and admirers have never given up on Aristotle. Whenever you hear, "Well, we just couldn't afford to build it," or "The rate of return was too low to go through with the project," or "Studies found the project to be economically unfeasible," or "The cost of labor was too high," or "The government should keep out of industry and agriculture because it distorts the sanctity and purity of the market," or "Yes, it's too bad, but we just had to cut those people off for unavoidable economic reasons," or "Sorry, your fate is just a reflection of the market finding a new equilibrium," or "Yes, we used to do great things, but now we just don't have the money," or "Science threatens to take away jobs"—stop and think. This poppycock was all overturned by Cusa, the man who initiated the project adopted by Columbus, to sail west to reach China in order to better link the East and West.

In Xi's China, and increasingly around the world, Aristotelian dogma is losing influence. Cusa's scientific method has growing influence. For example, the fact that the rapid, fairly unregulated growth of industry in China has led to very serious pollution problems, is not taken to mean that industry must be shuttered, and Africans told to give up the idea of ever having air conditioning (infamous initiatives of President Obama). A large productive population and clean air and water are not mutually exclusive. You just have to advance to the next step, the next level.

So, instead of promoting suicide, China is pushing to get beyond the problems of chemically fueling society, by hastening the development and deployment of nuclear fission and fusion, along with the electrification of everything that can be electrified.

For example, China has taken the world lead in the production of electric vehicles (ebikes, autos, and buses). It is the only country with commercially operating maglev rail systems. Already having the largest electricity generation capacity in the world, it is currently building twenty nuclear fission plants and has many more planned, and plans to export nuclear power plants of its own design and manufacture.

Just listing the statistics about China's rapid growth in all areas would astonish you.

Xi's Outlook

Xi invented the term "Chinese Dream." As with Cusa's coincidence of opposites, the Chinese Dream looks for the value in combining or bridging apparent contradictions between East and West, North and South, the rural farmer and the city factory worker; between Western music and traditional Chinese music; between modern medicine and traditional Chinese medicine, as with the recent Nobel prize for a malaria treatment derived from an ancient Chinese remedy. At the same time that it encourages its own population to master spoken and written Mandarin, it promotes the study of the English language by all of its students. There are 300 million students of the English language in China!

The Chinese Dream blankets the country from one end to the other with credit for good ideas (what Xi calls innovation). The source of wealth is the human mind, but it must be provided with credit to bring the ideas to fruition. If you have the work requirements and you have the people, it is credit that brings the two together. As Hamilton understood, it enables the future to pay for the present by massively increasing the power of the future—to the point that repaying the debt is a relatively minor undertaking compared to the increased productive power that the credit enabled to be created.

With Xi's announcement of the Belt and Road Initiative in 2013, China began the process of working with partner nations to create many new international development banks (along the lines of LaRouche's 1975 proposal for an International Development Bank), to finance global development with methods similar to those which have been, and are being used in China itself. Among these are the Asian Infrastructure Investment Bank (AIIB), the New Development Bank, and the Silk Road Fund.

Xi understands that it is credit that can bring together the requirements of the future and the unemployed hands of the present—credit that pays for the present by creating the future. That is the critical ingredient recently wiped out in the Western world. As in China, in the Western world there are millions of people with great potentials in their mental powers, but with no way to bring their potentials to reality as long as all credit goes to Wall Street and London predators.

It is high time that the United States overthrew the destructive domination of America by predatory Wall Street bankers, by reinstating Glass-Steagall and implementing the full Four Laws of LaRouche. With any significant agreement between Xi and Trump to bring the United States into the global BRI project, the pressure for the Four Laws will increase to an overwhelming degree, over and above the demands from Puerto Rico, Texas, Florida, and California. No solution but LaRouche's exists. China has proven that it works!

China's Auto Industry, Its Industrial Robots, and Automaker Chery

China's "Made in China 2025" strategy, with its emphasis on quality manufacturing, has given a tremendous boost to automation in China's industrial production. Rising labor costs have helped turn China into the world's largest consumer of industrial robots. The result is visible in the auto industry, which accounts for 42% of China's industrial robot use (the electronics industry comes second with 22%). The widespread use of automation and emphasis on innovation have brought China's auto industry to a level of quality comparable with that of Europe and Japan. In a test drive organized by Global Broadcasting Times for Chinese automaker Chery, on Sept. 25-26 in Germany, that quality was clearly demonstrated.

EIR was one of two western media invited to a two-day test drive and photo-shoot experience with the Tiggo 5x—the newest crossover (mini-SUV) by Chery. EIR's driver took the front-wheel drive, 1.5 liter turbo out on Autobahns and country roads, and into heavy city traffic. His impression was very favorable, finding the car's performance, comfort, passive and active safety systems, and generous range of options to be comparable to current western standards. The targeted market for this model is the younger generation. The large, intuitive touch-screen easily activates functions ranging from navigation, to weather forecasts, to web news. All touch-screen actions, and more, including starting the engine, can be activated using an app on your smartphone. Voice commands are recognized in all world languages and dialects!

Aaron Cao, marketing director of Market Research & Branding for Chery cars—who led the test group of fourteen, with four vehicles, through German cities, tourist sites, and vinyard country—explained that for Chery it is important to test the reaction of the German public. The German auto industry has been chosen as the benchmark by China, and Chery came to the Frankfurt International Auto Show not so much to market its cars—this will take a few more years—but to gauge the reactions and acceptance of German experts and consumers, confident that it can play this back into China to advantage.

Chinese cars of the Chery quality have a lot of western (German) engineering inside. Electrical components are manufactured by Bosch, while the transmission is by Getrag—two top producers for German and international automakers. The model we drove, with 147 horsepower, full leather seats, and a panoramic roof, sells in China for the equivalent of 13,000 Euro ($15,295), an "affordable" price, and indeed nearly a dumping price in Europe. However, if and when the car is sold in Europe, the price will be significantly higher.

Large metropoles such as Beijing suffer from traffic congestion and have introduced a ceiling on car ownership. Such limits on ownership in large cities are not a source of concern for China's auto industry, however. The government encourages driving since development is not limited to the big cities. In the countryside, living spaces are larger and further apart, and individual driving is therefore necessary.

Thus, the Chinese auto industry is rapidly expanding. China has been the largest automaker in the world when measured by unit production since 2008, and since 2009, annual production of

automobiles in China has exceeded that of the European Union, the United States, and Japan, combined. In 2014, total vehicle production in China reached 23.7 million, accounting for 26% of global automotive production. But that is not all. McKinsey, the global management consulting firm, estimates that by 2020 there will be 200 million vehicles on the road in China, which is one car for every seven Chinese. And there is much growth potential, when compared to the United States, where the ratio is one-to-one.

China wants to cover most of its growing internal market with automobiles produced in China. Standards for crash-testing, emissions, and reliability have been set and are rapidly being met.

Plant automation has played a major role in improving production quality. Today, robots put in screws more exactly than a worker can do with a screw driver, and robots do so in a fraction of the time. While still importing most of its robots from Japan and Europe, China has also begun to build its own robots. According to technical journals, China's robots still have some catching up to do, in terms of quality and reliability. However, in the long run, there is no doubt that the quality and performance of China's domestically produced robots will rise to the highest of international standards.

Meanwhile some companies are accelerating the automation process by acquiring western technology. A case that made international headlines was the acquisition of 95% of the leading German robot producer KUKA by the Chinese home appliances producer Midea at the end of last year. The acquisition was seen as a threat by European China-bashers, who are looking for pretexts to damage or stop cooperation with China. The European Union recently launched a mechanism to watch and eventually stop so-called "unfair" Chinese competition by using European government-sponsored or government-subsized companies to take over European firms of "strategic interest."

In the case of KUKA, however, the alarm were entirely bogus. Midea is a private Chinese company, quoted on the stock market, and the deal was entirely within the canonical "free-market" rules. As KUKA CEO Till Reuter said, in an interview with the Augsburger Allgemeine last January 20, "KUKA robots are now a strong division within the Midea family. Our aim is to make the KUKA brand, backed by its strong partner Midea, number one in the Chinese robot and automation market."

And the market is huuuuuuge…..

Almost one third (27%) of the world's industrial robots are currently sold in China. The demand is surging as China extends automation in the manufacturing sector. According to the International Federation of Robotics, this percentage will rise to 40% by 2019. Despite such large numbers, the density of robots in China is comparatively low at 49 per 10,000 workers, below the global average of 66. The KUKA-Midea potential will surely not be able to fill the gap alone.

The Fight Is On for South American Bioceanic Railway

by Gretchen Small

Oct. 30—China is inviting Ibero-America and the Caribbean to "get aboard China's high-speed development train," Zhang Run, Deputy Director General of the Latin American and Caribbean Affairs Department at the Chinese Foreign Ministry, announced in a press briefing in Beijing on Oct. 20. He added that "the Latin American and the Caribbean region is like an extension of China's Silk Road project, and we are ready to get more deeply involved."

Discussions are underway across the region on all kinds of individual projects as part of that offer, but none is more important than the construction of a bioceanic railway across the heart of the South American continent, connecting its Atlantic and Pacific coasts.

Since the first detailed discussion of such a rail line in the 1880s and 1890s under the impetus of the great development advocate U.S. Secretary of State James Blaine, this transcontinental railway has been recognized as the necessary platform for opening up the still-underpopulated, undeveloped interior of South America, transforming the entire continent into a modern economic powerhouse.

The Schiller Institute argued the urgency of building two bioceanic rail lines across the heart of South America—as well as critical North-South routes to link South America to North America, through the Darien Gap—in its 1986 book, *Ibero-American Integration: One Hundred Million New Jobs by 2000!* (serialized in English in

EIR at the time). That study, applying Lyndon LaRouche's method of physical economy, elaborated how the region can form an Ibero-American Common Market to counter the onslaught of neoliberal usury and new Opium Wars from which the Ibero-American and

Alternative Routes for South American Transcontinental Railroad

Source: *EIR.*

Caribbean nations have yet to be freed. The study outlined the integrated continental rail and water transport network capable of sustaining the great industrial and agricultural projects required to lift *all* the people of the region out of poverty—which today can be realized.

The decision to actually build the bioceanic rail lines is yet to be taken. Which route across the central heart of the continent should be built first, is still under discussion, while the governments of the two necessary bookends of such a railroad, Peru and Brazil, are (at best) dragging their feet, saying "yes," but looking to Wall Street for favors, unwilling to move.

China's offer to Ibero-America to join in sharing in its own stunning development through the Belt and Road Initiative (BRI), however, has stirred up a thirst for development, and an optimism that the region can finally take off. The power of this optimism is growing, overcoming the fear of bankrupt Wall Street thuggery.

The Bolivian government is playing a particularly important role in pushing this process forward, which, with the momentum provided by China, is leading to serious discussion of this great project, which is taking on a life of its own in South America, as never before. In the "new era" of development exploding around the world triggered by the Belt and Road, *EIR* is confident the obstacles can be overcome.

In fact, with even West Europeans joining China by bidding to play a part in this great project, it is beginning to look like the only nation *not* jumping at the chance to participate in making it a reality is the United States, whose policy for the region is still shaped too much by London's Wall Street. Abraham Lincoln, Blaine, William McKinley, and JFK would be as disgusted at today's short-sighted U.S. politicians and businessmen, as Lyndon LaRouche's magazine is!

If China Can End Poverty...

China's economic relations with Ibero-America have taken off. In his briefing to the press, Zhang Run reported that Ibero-America and the Caribbean are now the second-biggest regional destination for Chinese overseas investment, at 15% of all investment abroad, second only to its investments in Asia. Other Chinese officials have recently stated that China is involved in more than 179 specific projects in the region already, as Mexico's official news agency, Notimex, reported on Oct. 27.

Since 2015, Chinese investments in Brazil have increased by $19 billion, so that China is now Brazil's number one source of foreign investment, desperately needed when Brazil's national industrial and logistics capabilities are otherwise being dismantled by Wall Street's "anti-corruption" hit-squad known as *Lava Jato*.

Trade relations have grown to such an extent that now Argentina, Brazil, and Chile, together, provide 20-25% of all food imported by China, as Chile's Ambassador to China, Jorge Heine, reported in an Oct. 23 op-ed in China's *Global Times*. He called it "amazing" that Chile is now "the No. 1 exporter of fruit to China, with $1.2 billion [per year], meaning that one out of every four pieces of fruit imported by China by value ($5 billion) came from Chile, the farthest country from China."

China's development model is becoming as important as its resources in the region.

According to the World Bank, in 2015, one out of every five of the almost 648 million people living in Ibero-America and the Caribbean lived in chronic poverty (never escaping from it); that is 130 million people. Adding in the "transitory poor" (those driven into poverty supposedly temporarily), the number of poor is over 160 million, one in four. If anything, that number has grown since 2015, with the number of poor in Brazil alone rising by over one million since 2016, under Wall Street's grip, while the same policies are also increasing poverty rapidly in Argentina.

Thus, there is intense interest in China's success in lifting more people out of poverty over the last 30 years—700 million—than the entire population of Ibero-America and the Caribbean, and doing so by focusing on infrastructure, and technological and scientific advance.

The Executive Secretary of the UN's Economic Commission for Latin America and the Caribbean (ECLAC), Alicia Bárcenas, was interviewed by Xinhua on Oct. 18 after President Xi Jinping's opening report to the 19th National Congress of the Communist Party of China. She noted how "impressed" she is at what China has accomplished in the five years of Xi Jinping's presidency, by improving the quality of life of its people, including pulling nearly 60 million out of poverty. China's world leadership has been achieved by "innovation, the platform which has brought about the great modernization of China," and provided the Chinese people "greater opportunities, intellectually and even in questions of jobs," she said.

Bárcenas called for the region to put aside internal conflicts, and get to work on drafting a unified proposal for the infrastructure, science, technology, and innovation projects which should be incorporated in the 2019-2021 China-Latin America Caribbean Action Plan. Relations with China would be facilitated if it dealt with a regional bloc, rather than 33 different nations, she argued.

One of the tunnels of the Coca Codo Sinclair hydroelectric project in Napo province, Ecuador, being built by Sinohydro Corporation of China. It is the biggest hydroelectric power station on the Amazon River in Ecuador.

The Belt and Road Factor

The sheer scope of the Belt and Road Initative (BRI) is encouraging more audacious regional thinking throughout Ibero-America.

Uruguay is one country enthusiastically urging others to join it in jumping onboard the BRI. Antonio Carámbula, Executive Director of Uruguay's trade and investment promotion agency, Uruguay XXI, has been traveling throughout the region, promoting participation in this year's Nov. 30-Dec. 2 meeting of the "China-Latin America & Caribbean" (China-LAC) business summit in Punta del Este, Uruguay. Its two main panels will be on the BRI, and on cooperation on development and infrastructure. The BRI "is shaking the world," he said in a visit to Panama last week. (This forum meets annually, sponsored by the Chinese Council for the Promotion of International Trade (CCPIT) and the Inter-American Development Bank.)

Chile's former President Eduardo Frei, now Minister Plenipotentiary for Asia-Pacific Affairs in the Bachelet government, told an Aug. 30 seminar in Beijing on "Chile and the Belt and Road Initiative," that his government seeks to fully participate in the BRI, and especially to form joint ventures with Chinese companies to build infrastructure in Chile. Chile wants to "access new technologies" offered by China in order to industrialize; "we don't just want to be permanent raw materials exporters," Frei told EFE news service while in Beijing.

In an Oct. 9 interview with *China Hoy*, Chile's Un-dersecretary of Public Works, Sergio Galilea, specified two southern bioceanic corridors between Chile and Argentina that Chile wants China to help build. The more difficult is the two-way tunnel beneath the snowy Agua Negra pass, high in the Andes. "It's not just anyone who can build tunnels at 4,500 meters of altitude," Galilea noted.

Enter Bolivia

"The Latin American nations, Bolivia among them, are today a natural extension of what is called the '21st Century New Silk Road'," Bolivia's official ABI news agency wrote on Oct. 24, in reporting about the upcoming Nov. 9-11 "International China-LAC Expo" in Guangdong, China.

Since it nationalized the oil and gas industry in 2006, when Bolivia was one of the three poorest nations in the Americas, President Evo Morales's government has set out to create the industrial base and infrastructure required for Bolivia to become a modern nation employing 21st Century technology. This includes arranging training for a small cadre force of nuclear and aerospace engineers and technicians.

Receiving only hostility from the still British/Wall Street-dominated United States, Bolivia found allies in Russia, China, and some other Asian nations for its development.

China's Ambassador to Bolivia, Liang Yu, was emphatic in an Oct. 2 interview with the Bolivian daily *El Deber*, that China intends to "energetically" help Bolivia, in any way Bolivia wishes, to develop into a prosperous, industrial nation at the center of a prosperous and developing South America.

"Expanding cooperation on such areas as productive capacity, mining and energy, infrastructure, the development of highways, airports, railroads and hydroelectric plants, and collaboration and exchanges in such areas as aerospace, telecommunications, science and technology, and protection of the environment, will drive the development of Bolivian industrialization; the value-added of Bolivian products will increase, and its capacity for autonomous development will advance," Ambassador Liang told the daily.

Bolivia's President Evo Morales (L) and Wu Yanhua, a representative of the China Aerospace Science and Technology Corporation, hold a miniature model of the "Tupak Katari" communications satellite.

He cited in particular, the contract signed for China's Sinosteel Equipment and Engineeering Co. to build a steel complex near Bolivia's huge Mutun iron ore deposits, which when completed—projected now for 2020—will turn Bolivia into a significant steel producer in Ibero-America. Today it produces no steel to speak of.

Ambassador Liang rightly called the Mutun steel complex "a gigantic step for the industrialization of Bolivia." Mutun has some of the largest and purest iron ore (and manganese) deposits in the world, and the government has long sought to create a pole of development based on processing that ore. Sinosteel's contract is to build an iron ore concentration plant, a pelletizing plant, a direct reduction plant, and a steelworks with a continuous caster and a rolling mill, such that Bolivia can become largely self-sufficient in sponge iron, structural steel and "long products" (bars, rods, beams and rails).

Eventually, Bolivia will become a steel exporter, after the second phase of the project is completed, including construction of the necessary logistical capabilities for export (roads, bridges, railways, and port infrastructure).

And the Bioceanic Railway

Bolivia's idea is to turn its geographic position at the center of the South American continent into an asset, transforming itself into an energy and transport hub for the continent, making this the key to its entire industrial development project.

In 2010, Bolivian President Evo Morales proposed a bioceanic railway to Peru's then-President Alan García.

But what turned the bioceanic railway into an actual possibility was China's commitment to see one built. In meetings on the sidelines of the 2014 BRICS summit in Fortaleza, Brazil, President Xi reached agreements with the then-Presidents of Brazil and Peru to cooperate on building a bioceanic railway. Bolivia immediately began organizing for the bioceanic rail line to pass through its territory as well.

Since then, two primary routes have been contending for the project. Few are bold enough to recognize that the Schiller Institute is right, that if the trans-Atlantic sector—including South America—joins the physical economic cooperation proposed in the Belt and Road, and, like China, commits to eradicating *all* poverty within their nations, then both routes, and more, will be needed to support the explosion of city-building and productive activity that will result.

The route recommended by China Railway Eryuan Engineering Group Co. (CREEC), in its feasibility study presented to the governments of Brazil and Peru in October 2016, would run from Brazil's Atlantic port of Santos into Peru, where it would cross the Andes at their lowest point in the north at Saramirisa, and end in one of Peru's Pacific ports, such as Paita. This northern route avoids the greater geological difficulties of the higher portions of the Andes mountains to the south.

At the initiative of the Economists Association of Peru's Ucayali region, a movement of business, labor, indigenous, and civic representatives from the northwest of Peru is determined that this northern route be built, as it passes through their region. In November 2016, the Ucayali group made the Brazil-Peru bioceanic railway development corridor the central topic of the national Economists Association annual convention, and invited German Schiller Institute president Helga Zepp-LaRouche to give the keynote speech. The movement has drafted proposals for bringing supporting infrastructure, science cities, industry, and development into the largely undeveloped Amazon region, and has not stopped holding meetings and organizing since.

The other proposed route is the Central Bioceanic Railway Corridor championed by the Bolivian government. This would run from the port of Santos, through

Bolivia Communications Ministry

On the location of the huge Mutun iron ore deposit in Bolivia.

the bioceanic railway. It is said that the total amount of investment for this megaproject is enormous, and concerns numerous countries. When the work is completed, it will facilitate the exchange of the region's goods and people, and efficiently promote the ecnomic development of all the countries through which it passes. China is waiting for the interested countries to carry out a feasibility study of the project, laying a solid basis for the later execution of the project.

Bolivia, into southern Peru, where it would terminate at the Pacific port of Ilo. Bolivia proposes that six of South America's 12 nations would benefit, if the Brazil-Bolivia-Peru bioceanic rail corridor were connected to the Paraná-Paraguay waterway, which would incorporate Argentina, Uruguay, and Paraguay. That can easily be accomplished by running a rail line down from the Bolivian portion of the bioceanic line, to a Paraguayan port on the waterway.

Bolivia is lining up interested nations to sign memoranda of understanding on the project, and has set up a technical working group. Bolivian Foreign Minister Fernando Huanacuni has stated several times that ideological differences among governments in South America cannot be allowed to get in the way of getting this project built.

German, Swiss, Austrian, Italian, and Spanish companies, some with the active backing of their governments, are also making offers for how they could participate.

For its part, the Bolivian Ministry of Public Works signed an agreement with the Military Engineering School earlier this month to begin training rail experts. And, as occurred along the northern route, cities through which the railroad would pass (e.g. Bolivia's Cochabamba and Oruro, and Peru's Arequipa and Ilo) are already discussing preparations for the changes it could bring.

In this hot debate over routes, China has made clear it is open to both, but is waiting for the countries in the region to make their decision. China's Ambassador Liang told *El Deber*:

China is paying attention to the construction of

Political Will Accomplishes Dreams

What has seriously set back the great project, is Wall Street's two *de facto* coups in 2016 in two key countries: in Brazil (with the ouster of President Dilma Rousseff, placing subservient Michel Temer in office) and in Peru (placing Boston banker Pedro Pablo Kuczynski in the presidency).

PPK (as Kuczynski is known) rejected the northern route flat-out on monetarist grounds (too expensive!) and environmentalist excuses (can't touch the Amazon!). The seriousness of his current stated support for the central route, remains to be tested. Brazil's actual position is also unclear. Although the government is said to be about to give a formal "yes" to proceeding on feasibility studies for the central route, Temer (who has a 3% popularity rating) has been abjectly loyal to Wall Street's hatred of such projects, and is likely to remain so.

But because neither China, nor Bolivia, nor many in Peru accept "no" for an answer, organizing for the project has never stopped.

Bolivian Deputy Minister of Planning and Strategy, Hianny Rubén Romero, hit the nail on the head when he told a Paraguay seminar on South American infrastructure for regional integration on Oct. 24, that "political will" is often "a factor which can determine whether any such project is done or not done."

Bolivia wants to "dream big" about functioning as "the heart of South America" with the railway uniting the continent's two coasts. "Many dreams which were seen as impossible have been realized," he said. "Sometimes one may think that a project is very ambitious, and it can be ruled out as not feasible, but when there is will, enthusiasm, and technical competence by the different countries, it is simply a matter of putting it on the agenda, and aligning interests."

Yemen Victim of UN's Regime Change Policies

Oct. 21—The Tehran-based news agency Tasnim ran an interview Oct. 21 with EIR's Stockholm correspondent Ulf Sandmark. A slightly edited transcript is republished below with permission of Tasnim.

The following is the full text of the interview.

Tasnim: As a human rights activist, what do you think about the ongoing human tragedy in Yemen, caused by the Saudi blockades on the country's ports and airspace? The Red Cross has warned that cholera, a diarrheal disease that has been eradicated in most developed countries, could infect a million people in Yemen by the end of the year, according to media reports. Why have the international organizations, particularly the UN, remained passive in the face of the ongoing Saudi atrocities?

Ulf Sandmark: Thank you for the question. My point is that the international organizations have too limited an agenda to stop the war. Their agenda is to alleviate the suffering and describe what is going on. It is good as far as it goes, but what is needed are political actions, which could only be demanded from governments, politicians, political organizations, and citizens acting politically. Such needed action, we see now, for example, from the four U.S. Congressmen forcing a vote in Congress against the U.S. support of the war on Yemen.

The UN should be able to act, but is too much dominated by the modern form of British empire, with its Commonwealth members and the Western allies. The UN has even backtracked on its Westphalian Peace conceptions of national sovereignty and adopted the regime-change agenda of Tony Blair, the so-called R2P ["responsibility to protect"]. Yemen is a victim of the regime-change policies. The main formerly warring

Ulf Sandmark

Ulf Sandmark is a Swedish economist and human rights activist as well as a longtime collaborator of American political figure Lyndon H. LaRouche. Sandmark is a board member of the Schiller Institute in Sweden and the Stockholm correspondent for the Executive Intelligence Review (EIR). As a child, he lived for three years with his family in Addis Ababa, and became active in Third World development issues at the time of his studies at the Stockholm School of Economics. He has written many articles and proposals for development programs, including

"The Phoenix Program—Discussion Points for the Reconstruction of Syria" (co-author Hussein Askary) about how to realize the major potential for recovery in linking up Syria to the New Silk Road. As a chairman of the Anti-Drug Coalition in Sweden for twenty years, he has written about how to dismantle the drug banks and their narco-terrorist bands. He has also delivered speeches at various international conferences, including a two-day conference held in London last year to "support the Yemeni people against the Anglo-American-Saudi imperial war."

Yemeni factions, the Ansarullah Movement and the party of the former President, Ali Abdullah Saleh, had joined together to form an independent Yemeni national leadership in early Spring 2015, into which also other political parties joined. This new leadership of Yemen was outside the control of the Anglo-Americans and their puppet Saudi Arabia, who started the illegal war against Yemen to reverse that.

Tasnim: As you may know, airstrikes by the Saudi-led coalition have killed mostly Yemeni civilians, including thousands of women and children. A recent report authored by several international aid agencies said Yemen suffered more airstrikes in the first half of this year than in the whole of 2016, increasing the number of civilian deaths and forcing more people to flee their homes. In your opinion, why has the Saudi regime decided to increase the airstrikes, hitting civilian targets?

Sandmark: Militarily, the Saudi-led coalition is losing the war and cannot move their forces into Yemen without being repelled. They are only able to try to break the will of their enemy by attacking the population. However, there is more to this, as the Saudi air force is also attacking the culture and heritage of Yemen. What we see are the same Dark Age forces destroying other nations in the region. The policy is not to conquer, but to block development and create lawless regions, which can be centers of destabilizations of the entire Eurasian continent. As in Idlib province in Syria, where whole villages are taken over and used as training camps for terrorists from the minorities from Western China.

The British empire is, as always, too weak to rule without other people as their tools. They do not have military forces, even with the help of the United States, to take on nations like Iran, much less India, China or Russia. Their chosen option has been to foment internal destabilization among the hundreds of minorities of Eurasia, to block the emerging economic and political power of the BRICS and the Silk Road Initiative.

As Syria is about to reassert its sovereignty, and even Somalia is approaching peace, there is an urgent need by the British troublemakers to tear down Yemen into a Dark Age region where terrorists can be trained, especially in such a strategic area between Africa and Asia, close to the maritime Silk Road.

Tasnim: Recently-leaked emails written by two former top U.S. officials have shown that Saudi Arabia's crown prince and defense minister, Mohammed bin Salman, "wants out" of the war he started in Yemen. The Saudi regime has reached none of its objectives in Yemen. In 2015, the kingdom had a record budget deficit of almost $100 billion, prompting it to rein in public spending in a bid to save money. Why is the regime continuing its attacks on Yemen despite its failures and cash-strapped economy? What do you think about the future of the war?

Sandmark: The Saudis were recruited by the British Empire in the 18th Century and elevated to rule in the style of the Maharajas of East India Company rule. They are not allies, but just tools of the empire. The young Salman evidently did not understand this, and started a war that could destroy the rule of the Saudi family. Now he is locked into the war and cannot stop it. The British interest is to foment chaos, and clearly, not to stop him from destroying himself. In the meantime, they just steal money from the Saudis, just as many others do.

The chaos in the Persian Gulf states is targetting the great emerging Asian nations, especially China, who depend on the oil from there. Russia depends on the oil price. As China and Russia, and their allies in Asia, are clearly threatened by chaos in the Persian Gulf, [this broader conflict] limits their ability to stop the Yemen war. They are trying to bring the Saudis to a peace policy by inviting them into the New Silk Road Initiative, but Salman canceled all Saudi infrastructure projects in the economic plan. What would solve the situation is to end British colonialism on the Arabian Peninsula, and let their peoples create republics oriented to the development of their citizens.

In the meantime, the British and their evil geopolitics must be attacked and isolated. The responsibility for the creation of the greatest human catastrophe in the world just now must be put squarely on the shoulders of the British and their main allies, the U.S. and France. The brutal war on Yemen must stop immediately. It is not permissible to use a UN Resolution to commit crimes against humanity.

President Trump in China: Picking up John F. Kennedy's Torch

by Dennis Speed

Oct. 31—The Oct. 26 release by President Trump of large sections of the still-classified files on the assassination of President John F. Kennedy has usefully forced into view not only the matter of the "Kennedy coverup," but more important, the significance of the aborted Kennedy Presidency. "Who shot JFK?" remains an important question, but "what is the significance of what has happened to the United States since the death of JFK?" is a far more important one.

The month of November will feature both the trip of President Trump to Asia, and the 54th anniversary of the JFK assassination. This is also the centennial of John Kennedy's birth (on May 29, 1917). It might have been expected, especially given the identification of Baby-Boomers with JFK, that the last six months would have featured extensive commemorations of the martyred President; instead, there have been few. This may be because, in the face of the challenges that JFK posed to Americans—including the elimination of poverty in the United States by the end of the century, seventeen years ago—most would prefer not to evaluate honestly "how we've done."

Now, the prospect proposed by China's President Xi Jinping—and implicitly by the great opportunity that is being presented to President Trump—is that of the United States working closely with the 1.4 billion-person nation of China, a nation that has lifted 700 million of its citizens out of poverty, and vows to lift everyone in that nation (and even, with other nations' help, much of the world) out of poverty within the next ten years, through the "win-win" Belt and Road Initiative (BRI). This return to physical productivity, using FDR's crash program methods, and JFK's "Apollo Project" model as well, can allow the United States to return to the quality of world leadership that JFK aspired to.

In his 2004 essay, "The Coming Eurasian World," Lyndon LaRouche states: "In an existential crisis, such as the present world situation, which has those or similar attributes of a threatened general breakdown of the system, the danger comes chiefly from the leadership which fails to break with the pre-established policy-shaping trends, the failure to break in the way President Franklin Roosevelt did in his 1932 election-campaign, and in the turnabout in U.S. policy which he introduced beginning the first hours in the Administration." Such a seismic shift in American foreign and domestic policy could, and should occur in the month of November. That, rather than nostalgia or tearful remembrance of what might have been, is the proper context for this brief consideration of America's potential next decade, from JFK's standpoint.

A New Frontier for All of Humanity

Once, during his Administration's first year, President John Kennedy asked the Joint Chiefs of Staff to brief him on the battle plan for thermonuclear war. After initially refusing, the generals briefed Kennedy on the Joint Strategic Capabilities Plan to drop 170 such weapons on the city of Moscow alone. Kennedy turned to another person present, and remarked: "And we call ourselves the human race." Despite the anti-human Bertrand Russell and others' attempts to disorient him, Kennedy, acting as a sovereign President, stood fast against "the doomsday faction" and avoided thermonuclear holocaust in October 1962.

Having successfully reversed the world's near-destruction, through the efforts of his brother Robert and representatives of the Soviet administration that negotiated with him through a "back channel" on behalf of Nikita Khrushchov, Kennedy later proposed at the United Nations General Assembly on Sept. 20, 1963, a different vision for the two nations and for mankind.

If the Soviet Union and the United States, with all of their global interests and clashing commitments of ideology, and with nuclear weapons still aimed at each other today, can find areas of common interest and agreement, then surely other nations can do the same… in a field where the United States and the Soviet Union have a special capacity—in the field of space—there is room for new cooperation, for further joint efforts in the regulation and exploration of space. I include among these possibilities a joint expedition to the Moon. Space offers no problems of sovereignty; by resolution of this Assembly, the members of the United Nations have foresworn any claim to territorial rights in outer space or on celestial bodies, and declared that international law and the United Nations Charter will apply. Why, therefore, should man's first flight to the Moon be a matter of national competition? Why should the United States and the Soviet Union, in preparing for such expeditions, become involved in immense duplications of research, construction, and expenditure? Surely we should explore whether the scientists and astronauts of our two countries—indeed of all the world—cannot work together in the conquest of space, sending some day in this decade to the Moon not the representatives of a single nation, but the representatives of all of our countries.

President Trump's proposal to return America to a manned space program is one of the central planks of his "Make America Great Again" platform. This is not about space, but about the future of humanity, which includes the future of the United States. Most Americans are still unaware of Trump's statements on space exploration, but these are important, in that they indicate an impulse tendency on his part to "break with the previous policy trends" of the "double Bush" Administrations of 2001-2017. In contrast, Barack Obama's infamous shut-down of the American space program's Moon initiative, saying "we've already been there," and his British imperial approach to relations with China, came from the same "no-future outlook" which was the antithesis of the 200-plus years of American scientific and technological progress.

In remarks at his signing of an Executive Order on the National Space Council, President Trump stated on June 30 this year:

We're a nation of pioneers, and the next great

President John F. Kennedy with Secretary of Defense Robert S. McNamara, and Chairman of the Joint Chiefs of Staff, General Maxwell D. Taylor.

American frontier is space. And we never completed—we started, but we never completed. We stopped. But now we start again… Every launch into the skies is another step forward toward a future where our differences seem small against the vast expanse of our common humanity. Sometimes you have to view things from a distance in order to see the real truth. It is America's destiny to be at the forefront of humanity's eternal quest for knowledge, and to be the leader amongst nations on our adventure into the great unknown. And I could say the great and very beautiful unknown. Nothing more beautiful.

Those that have followed closely the intention of the Chinese to return the human race to the Moon, know why this may be another area in which President Trump and President Xi may seek common ground. Perhaps President Trump will discuss with China the prospect for joint American-Chinese—or even American-Chinese-Russian—projects to return to the Moon and to begin the process of mining helium-3 there. This would certainly recall JFK's 1963 United Nations initiative toward the then Soviet Union, designed to end war. At that time, Kennedy remarked, "I would say to the leaders of the Soviet Union, and to their people, that if either of our countries is to be fully secure, we need a much better weapon than the H-bomb—a weapon better than ballistic missiles or nuclear submarines—and that better weapon is peaceful cooperation."

While there are those that seek to compare Trump's trip to China, to that of Richard Nixon and Henry Kissinger in 1972, they fail to note that then China was in the throes of the Cultural Revolution, and was industrially backward; today, China is the world's leading industrial economy in fact, both from all physical-economic terms of measurement, and from the impulse-tendency for future economic growth through investment in new technologies and a skilled workforce. And beyond mere peaceful cooperation to prevent war—the best that JFK could hope for with the Soviet Union—the Chinese have made it abundantly clear that they wish to work with the United States as a full partner in the Belt and Road Initiative. To that end, economist Lyndon LaRouche and his associates wrote and released in 2014 the *EIR* Special Report, *The New Silk Road Becomes the World Land-Bridge,* thus making available to the American Presidency an advanced response to the September 2013 proposal by Xi Jinping that the United States join the Belt and Road Initiative and the BRICS alliance. The Obama Administration, however, was "unconstitutionally" incapable of responding to this, as they were incapable of responding to China. Now, as recently stated in the title of an editorial in China's *Global Times*, "China, America Can Be Great Together":

Managing the relationship of competitive coex-

istence between China and the U.S.A. could be becoming more difficult, but bilateral relations have been more stable since Trump took office. Xi and Trump have maintained effective communications. The leaders hope to avoid a trade war and prevent tensions on the Korean Peninsula from spiraling out of control.... The two countries also have a prospective future in energy cooperation, including liquefied natural gas, clean coal, and nuclear power. The Belt and Road initiative can boost Sino-U.S. relations, and better Asia-Pacific infrastructure will generate more space for trade. Asia will need up to $26 trillion for infrastructure in the next 15 years—a lucrative market for U.S. companies.

Let us hope that, with the combination of the Asia trip of President Trump, and the release of large portions of the Kennedy files, the New Frontier of which John F. Kennedy spoke, and into which mankind ventured, will be renewed as the "New Western Frontier"—China, and the prospect of a new world of American positive leadership for the benefit of all humanity, devoted to the discovery of "the great and beautiful unknown."

Creating a Public Credit System

The following is an edited transcript of excerpts of a presentation by EIR *Economics Editor Paul Gallagher, delivered to the La-Rouche PAC Manhattan meeting on Saturday, Oct. 21, 2017, followed by a question and answer period with the audience. A* video of the full presentation *is available.*

Question: Within weeks U.S. President Donald Trump and China President Xi Jinping could be discussing new economic arrangements. What kind of arrangements?

Gallagher: For fifty years there has been in America, not just in American government and decision-making, but an unpreparedness in the American economy. This has been getting worse and worse, a failure to build the kind of productive and protective infrastructure planned decades ago—but never built—in places such as the Texas Gulf Coast to protect the cities like Houston and Rockport. It was also planned in New York, as people there know, and was never built, so that the subways filled up with salt water. Meanwhile, China and Japan have been leading the world in productive and protective infrastructure, and Trump is going to visit both places and have summits with both leaders. They are not just building infrastructure, but also making technological breakthroughs in infrastructure building—as for example, the bridges built with techniques that have never been used before and spanning distances not previously possible. They have been doing this now for thirty to forty years extremely efficiently, building high-speed rail and other infrastructure. These breakthroughs could be brought into the design and engineering of the most important infrastructure projects in the United States on a large scale, such as the Gateway Project and the New York

cc/Ray Devlin

Lake Borgne Surge Barrier in New Orleans, protective infrastructure built after Hurricane Katrina caused $200 billion in destruction and 1,800 lives were lost.

Harbor sea gates and tunnel. This could be done in the context of the creation of a credit institution here in the United States which would fund such projects.

As we have been proposing now for some time, the best and grandest way for the United States to form such a credit institution for manufacturing and infrastructure,—which we have not had now since Franklin Roosevelt—the fastest way and the best way to do that would be to allow the holders of relatively long-term Treasury debt to trade that debt for equity in a new national infrastructure bank on favorable conditions to them with the guarantee of the Treasury—to participate also in the investment in such infrastructure projects here in the United States and also in joint projects as far afield as South America, Syria, Alaska, and the Bering Strait crossing. Nations where major projects have to be done could participate directly through helping to capitalize a national United States bank for infrastructure and manufacturing, and also through participating in the design teams and the engineering teams which would work on selecting projects and getting them engineered.

Western press desperately claims debt in China, taken to grow the productive economy, is dangerous, and could lead to an economic collapse.

I've discussed all this with officials from both China and Japan in Washington recently. I've had the opportunity to learn that both of those countries would be extremely interested in investing a portion of their very large holdings of our Treasury debt in the equity of such a bank in order to get things going here, and also to jointly cooperate on great infrastructure projects internationally. As one official said to me, "This could not be proposed to the United States *by* us; this would have to be proposed by the United States *to* us. However, I can tell you, we would be extremely interested immediately in doing exactly this." In addition to the issue of war and peace and the issue of strategic stability, those things could be on the agenda and could really begin to be worked out fairly quickly.

Speculative Debt

Two huge expansions of credit—that is, debt—have occurred over the past ten years. One has been by the major central banks of Japan, Europe, the United States; and the other by the People's Bank of China and the publicly held large commercial banks in China—their big five commercial banks. Both of those credit expansions have been huge. They are comparable, in the range of $15-20 trillion equivalent in each case. All of the discussions and all of the warnings coming out now are about what part of this debt is going to collapse.

As you may know, the majority of so-called financial experts in the media say that it is the Chinese credit expansion which is going to blow out. What is the truth of that statement? China's rapid economic expansion has been going on now for just about thirty years. China has a Glass-Steagall law; it is really the only major economy in the world which has a currently enforced Glass-Steagall law. It isn't called that officially, but it's called that in informal discussion among Chinese economists. Recently, it has been more strongly enforced because of challenges to it by the formation of what we call non-banks in China—what we might think of as hedge funds and private equity funds here. In the middle 1990s, when the major Chinese public commercial banks were formed through action of the People's Bank of China and through legislation, they were also separated and not allowed to participate in merchant banking activities, or investment banking activities, and have not been allowed to do that since that time.

Look now at the other credit expansion, the debt expansion which has taken place by the central banks of Japan, Europe, and the United States, created since 2010, only seven years ago. Seven trillion dollars in new corporate debt, which was more than a doubling in seven years in the United States; $1 trillion in new auto debt; $1 trillion in new credit card debt; $2 trillion in new household debt overall; $11 trillion of new debt in seven years. And that is not counting government debt, which has increased by $7 trillion, or student debt which has increased by $600 billion in that same period. The four big central banks—the Federal Reserve, the Bank of England, the Bank of Japan, and the European Central Bank—alone have bought $14 trillion of this debt during this time. That's called "quantitative easing." We're talking about currency that was printed by the Federal Reserve and the other central banks in order to directly transfer it to the major banks of those countries, which then in turn used it to create a now ten-year-long era of effectively zero percent interest rate

The precarious position of the speculative-debt dominated financial system in the West is beginning to dawn on people.

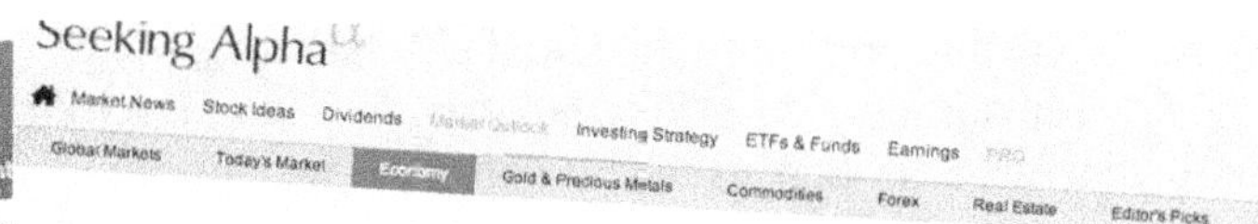

The Ultimate Debt Bubble Is Upon Us

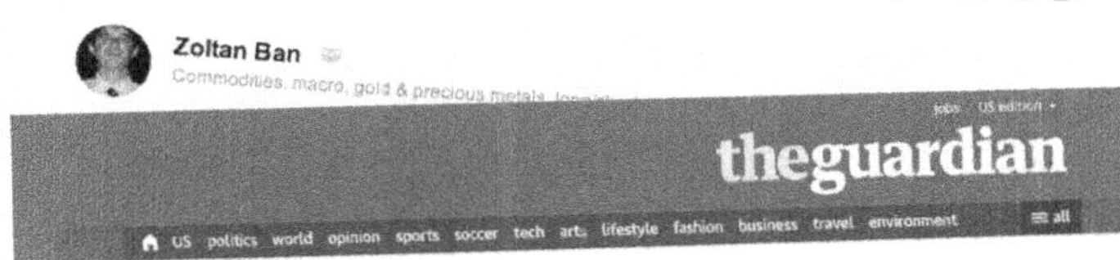

Borrowing & debt The Observer

Debt bubble returns millions to days of 2008 crash

Advisers call for action as growing numbers struggle with their bills

credit for speculation. That is, credit at 0% interest for the securities markets of the trans-Atlantic world.

For example, the Bank of Japan owns 75% of all of the exchange-traded funds on the Nikkei stock exchange—owns them. The Swiss National Bank owns $80 billion worth of U.S. stocks. The European Central Bank owns $90 billion of U.S. corporate bonds; many of which are below investment grade. The Federal Reserve owns $2.1 trillion of mortgage-backed securities—really derivatives—and $2.4 trillion in United States Treasuries, largely short-term Treasuries. This has made the price of debt close to zero if you're on the securities market, and if you are not dealing junk. But the share of what they call "junk debt" is growing, most especially in the U.S. corporate debt bubble. Recall the total bubble grew by $7 trillion since 2010; of that about $2.5 trillion is and has become junk debt. That means either junk bonds or what is termed leveraged loans— $800 billion in new junk debt just in 2017 through September. The rest of that corporate debt bubble, approximately 80% of it, the so-called "good debt," the non-junk debt being loaned at rates like 1% to the biggest corporations, has been thrown into the stock market.

Just this past Friday, Wells Fargo announced that it was being investigated both internally and also by Federal regulators for foreign exchange fraud. How many successive fraud cases and crimes does this make for Wells Fargo over the last year? Its stock went *up* on Friday after that announcement. General Electric announced revenue and profits for the quarter universally reported to be completely dismal; its stock went *up* for that day. The best example, perhaps, is a small company you may have heard of, ExxonMobil. In 2006, Exxon reported $365 billion in revenue. Eleven years later, it reported $226 billion in revenue—40% less. It reported profits in 2006 of $40 billion; in 2017, its profit was $7.8 billion—about 85% less. It reported in 2006 a free cash flow available to pay out to stockholders or to invest, of $33.8 billion. By 2017, that was down to $6 billion—one-sixth. It said it had $6.6 billion of debt back in 2006; In 2017, it had $29 billion in debt—five times as much. Its revenue dropped 40%; its profits and cash flow collapsed by more than 80%; its debt more than quadrupled. Yet, its stock price over that same period, went *up* from $75 to $90. How did ExxonMobil pull that off. It bought a modest 14 million shares of its own stock with the 0% credit that was being made available.

To stop all this is, first of all, we must immediately separate commercial banking from speculative investment banking and activities of hedge funds, such as issuance of derivatives, trading in commodities and foreign exchange indexes, and creation of asset-backed securities, so that these huge volumes of speculative debt which are now going bad cannot be dumped by the big banks onto pension funds and individual savers around the world. In other words, what they did in 2007-2008. Anyone who has seen the film "The Big Short" saw a demonstration of exactly how they did it. They are now doing the same thing with unpayable auto debt, unpayable corporate debt, and similar categories.

So, reinstating Glass-Steagall for one thing, will stop that process because it will not allow the bank holding companies to do this, to create the securities by which they're doing this.

Global Development: FDR and China

For the major central banks, this debt expansion added up to about $15 trillion. Put that $15 trillion in expansion of debt on top of no productivity growth. Since 2000, the average growth in labor productivity in the United States has been 0.5% per year. The average growth in what is called total factor productivity—a significantly more important measure I'll explain in a minute—has averaged 0.3% annual increase. Put $15 trillion in debt on top of that, and then look at the labor markets and what has happened to the labor forces in the United States and Europe.

In the United States in the 1980s and the 1990s, of the people who were newly eligible to enter the labor market during those two decades, about 75-80% *did* enter the labor market and *stayed* in it; they were still in it either working or looking for work at the end of that decade. In the decade from 2000 to 2010, of the potential eligible new entrants into the labor force during that decade, 30% actually entered the labor force and stayed in it. During the Obama Presidency, between 20-25% of the expansion of the labor force that could have occurred, actually occurred. So, there was a collapse in the quality of employment and in the portion of the labor force which was actually taking part in any way— this at the same time as this $15 trillion money printing was being thrown at the securities' markets, bringing them to the point of a crash.

Now keep in mind, President Trump came into office with the stated intention to fund $1 trillion worth of infrastructure building, and to do that at least in part from some kind of national bank or national fund. So, the big private equity companies on Wall Street— BlackRock, for example—set up an infrastructure fund; $50 billion they said was either in it or committed to it. Others on Wall Street did similar things, saying they had huge amounts of private capital ready to invest in infrastructure. But they had conditions, and they stated publicly what their conditions were: no less than a 10% annual return on their investment. This is while interest rates were between one and two percent on major corporate debt, and less than that for investments in stocks and securities and derivatives speculation. They wanted a 10% annual return, and also they wanted all of their invested capital back in ten years. Now compare that to China. In China, the government-to-government loans being made by the Chinese Ex-Im Bank, for example, and being made domestically and internationally by the other public commercial banks in China, are typically 30-year-pay-back loans at 1-2%. But in the United States, Wall Street's intention was to turn infrastructure investment into what they called "deep junk" debt; that was going to be how they would handle President Trump's intention to invest $1 trillion in infrastructure.

A lawyer I was talking to the other day, who used to be a Congressman from the Midwest, in a meeting discussing our national infrastructure bank proposal, asked me "What's Wall Street's view going to be on this? They're going to oppose it, right?" They are definitely opposing it, and going to oppose it, because we're putting Hamilton into infrastructure investment, and taking financier profit out of it. So, they are going to oppose that. Wall Street's policy is to pin Trump to this stock market boom which is actually getting ready to crash. Their policy is to make him own that stock market boom, identify with it, cut taxes to keep it going, and if there is any infrastructure investment, to put it in the framework of that junk debt.

China's debt expansion has been approximately the same magnitude; in fact, it may have been somewhat more new credit, new debt created through those public commercial banks in China. Two-thirds of the corporate debt in China, *two-thirds of all of it*, is concentrated in 22 companies. They are, all 22 of them, involved either entirely or to a very great degree in infrastructure building and in energy development. I'll just quote *Asia Times* for example in an analysis on Thursday: "A great deal of Chinese corporate indebtedness should be viewed as public works investments by the Chinese sovereign. The point to take away is that we are not looking at a speculative bubble in corporate debt, but at a heavily concentrated investment in state-sponsored infrastructure. Manufacturing, health care, and other major corporate sectors in China actually show declining debt leverage. The bulk of corporate debt has built up in energy production, power production, rail development, high-speed rail, airlines. Sectors that in many other countries would be funded directly via the state budget. China has been borrowing mainly to expand infrastructure." Rather surprisingly, the ratio of net debt to earnings of these 22 companies—they're all large companies, obviously—will fall from 3.71 in 2016 to

2.5; that is, they will be less leveraged with debt by a significant amount in 2017 and 2018 than they were in prior years. So, this $20 trillion debt expansion from China, if you call it that, over the past decade, is backed by at least $10 trillion in infrastructure, public assets alone. The firm of PricewaterhouseCoopers has done several recent studies this year, showing that the value of China's capital assets in infrastructure, in the Belt and Road countries, is rising by 40-50% every year, and is already in the order of hundreds of billions of dollars.

This, by the way, is what Lyndon LaRouche said in the 1950s and 1960s the United States should do. He was not just forecasting the breakup of the Bretton Woods system at that time. He was saying what had to be done, instead. He said that the United States, following its tremendous expansion in industrial production and productivity from the 1930s through World War II, should have continued that expansion after 1945 in the Third World. What America should have done was to transition from those huge investments in productivity in the United States, to the export of capital goods and infrastructure into what were then called the countries of the Third World—to have many Marshall Plans.

Just as people now compare the Belt and Road Initiative to 10 or 20 Marshall Plans, what LaRouche was saying in the 1950s and the 1960s was that such an expansion outward to the world as a whole was precisely what the United States should have done.

Instead, what the United States did, and Lyndon LaRouche was very ruthless on this in the '60s, in particular, was to invest in a big consumer boom. The Eisenhower Federal Reserve, under Arthur Burns and others, in Eisenhower's administration in particular, pushed U.S. credit policy instead towards a consumer boom: everything from second cars to lots of toys for the kids, to household appliances to hula hoops, and so forth—this was what was bought with the continuing credit expansion in the United States in the '50s and early '60s, till Kennedy broke with this. And that's exactly what LaRouche was attacking at that time, and that is exactly what the IMF—and all the others like it—are advising China to *do* right now.

These western "experts" say, "China should cut out this Belt and Road stuff; it's all very nice, it's harmonious for the world, but it's too much of a credit expansion in infrastructure. Instead they should be investing in increasing consumer consumption in China." But China is not interested in repeating the mistakes that the United States made in the 1950s.

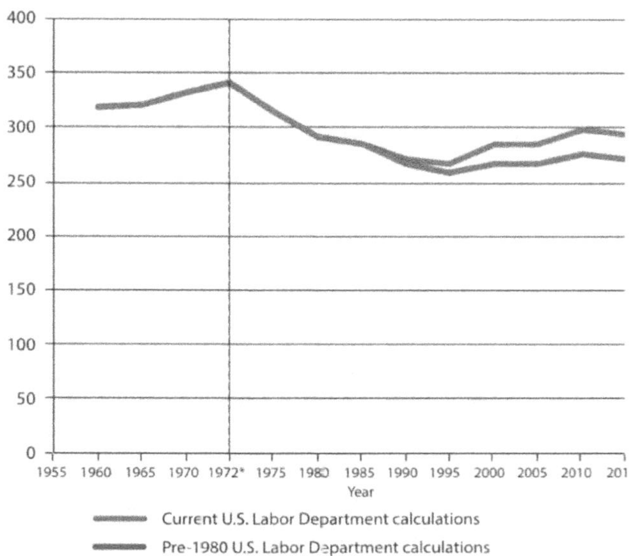

As *EIR* Washington Bureau Chief Bill Jones was saying in the webcast last night, China's global initiative was not by any means something that Xi Jinping simply proposed in late 2013, and everyone in the Chinese leadership said, "Oh, yes, of course. This is our fate. Our future is the Belt and Road Initiative." They did not. Many people, including some Chinese economists, have still been resisting the idea that the Belt and Road Initiative is the dynamic of the Chinese economy for the future, as well as the productive dynamic for the world economy for the future. And as Bill was saying, what you're seeing in the proceedings of the Chinese Communist Party Congress going on now, is a consolidation of that vision, as put forward four years ago by Xi Jinping.

Real Productivity

On the slide [**Figure 1**], the red line, beginning in 1970, shows the decline in median real weekly earnings of U.S. working people since that time. The blue line which branches off represents the fact that in the 1980s, as we exposed at that time, the U.S. government dramatically changed the way it was calculating inflation—and obviously inflation is one of the things determining real wages. If the government agency had kept the same measures defining inflation throughout, the graph would show an approximately 15-20% decline in the median real wage during this period.

De-industrialization was starting at that time,—the so-called Southern Strategy—eventually leading to a thorough de-industrialization of the United States and to the past 15 to 20 years' deadly opium and suicide epidemic among working age people in the formerly industrial areas of the United States. The space exploration program dramatically shrank by about 85%, in just three years, during the Vietnam War. No major infrastructure investment occurred in the United States for the next 45 years—none.

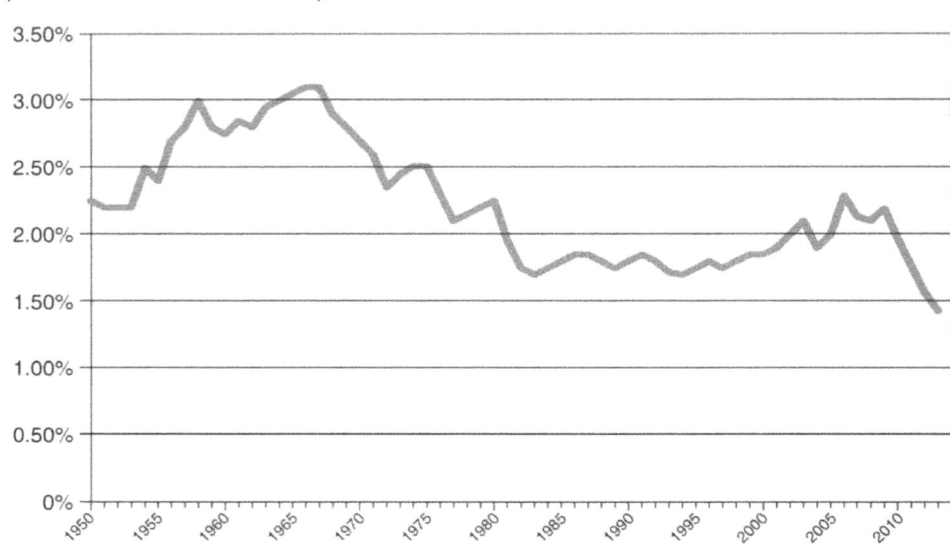

Recently, Helga LaRouche pointed out that this was also what her husband understood about the Soviet economy, when he made his famous forecast in 1983, that the Soviet system would collapse in five years—he missed it by one year—unless they accepted the major cooperative technology and infrastructure program known as the Strategic Defense Initiative, as a joint program of the United States and the Soviet Union. Lyndon LaRouche recognized that while the Soviet Union stressed both invention and scientific development, they did not invest in infrastructure. That was a complete blank, a zero in the Soviet economy. What investments were made were shoddy; the example of the Chernobyl nuclear plant for example, which was effectively the same as the 1941 atomic pile in Chicago, when Enrico Fermi and others were developing nuclear energy. It was the lack of infrastructure investment in the Soviet Union, which caused them to loot the countries of Eastern Europe and brought their system to collapse.

Our next slide [**Figure 2**] shows infrastructure investment as a percentage of GDP in the United States, going back to the 1950s. You can see how sharply infrastructure investment rose during the impulse of Kennedy's nuclear and water development, and the Apollo Program, and then how steadily it has fallen ever since then, to where it is now less than 1.5% of GDP. Compare that to China, where infrastructure investment is consistently 9% of GDP every year. These days, most investment in infrastructure in the United States now is done by municipalities, not by the federal government.

This next slide [**Figure 3**] is total factor productivity. Labor productivity, the way it is normally defined, is simply the total GDP, the total output, which could be anything, divided by the total number of hours worked by the workforce. That doesn't tell you much. Total factor productivity is something different: It's an index which attempts to measure the impact of technological advance on labor productivity. It's complicated, but it essentially looks at what has been wrought by technological advance on productivity in the economy.

You can see that there was a golden age of productivity in the United States, beginning with Roosevelt's 1930s, a decade that actually had the largest steady increase in technological productivity of any decade in American history. Studies on this period make absolutely clear that this rate of growth, which was in the order of 3-3.5% per year, was the result of the great projects in infrastructure of the New Deal, and the way in which those great projects challenged the companies that were working on them, just as we see in the Chinese bridge-building and so forth today. They challenged the companies working on the projects to develop completely new technological methods and inventions in order to carry them out. And the result of that—even more than the war mobilization of the

1940s—was the most rapid growth in technological productivity in the U.S. economy, at least in the period which this index measures.

By comparison, the National Bureau of Economic Research estimated in a study in 2014 that the rate of growth in total factor productivity in China's economy from 1999 to 2011 has been 3.11% annually. This is comparable to the golden age of productivity in the United States economy, not what you see after that. In the United States today, if you look at the period since 2010, you would be at zero total factor productivity, which is why the average since 2000 is below one-half of one percent.

Robert Gordon, a very famous economist, just wrote a book called *The Rise and Fall of American Growth*. It's all about total factor productivity. The most surprising thing he details there, is that the information technology (IT) revolution did not produce *any* growth in productivity at all! In May, the Organization of Economic Cooperation and Development, the OECD, put out a similar report and held a big conference in Paris about this. They said that the sectors directly related to IT is where the greatest *absence* of productivity growth was.

That is not the same as developing a crash program for fusion power; it's not the same as building high-speed rail; it's not the same as nuclear desalination. It does not protect cities on the Texas Gulf coast, and New York City, from devastation in hurricanes. It did not and does not have that effect.

Dialogue

Question: Please comment directly on Secretary of State Rex Tillerson's recent disparaging remarks on the China Belt and Road, specifically, his disparaging of the credit mechanism and the financing mechanism that he has done.

Gallagher: I mentioned ExxonMobil earlier, and what they have done to themselves since 2006. I think Tillerson was CEO at that time. And I think that what he said, what it represented, is the dominant Wall Street financial economist's view of how economic growth takes place.

It's completely, totally wrong. I don't necessarily think you have to assume that Tillerson was somehow

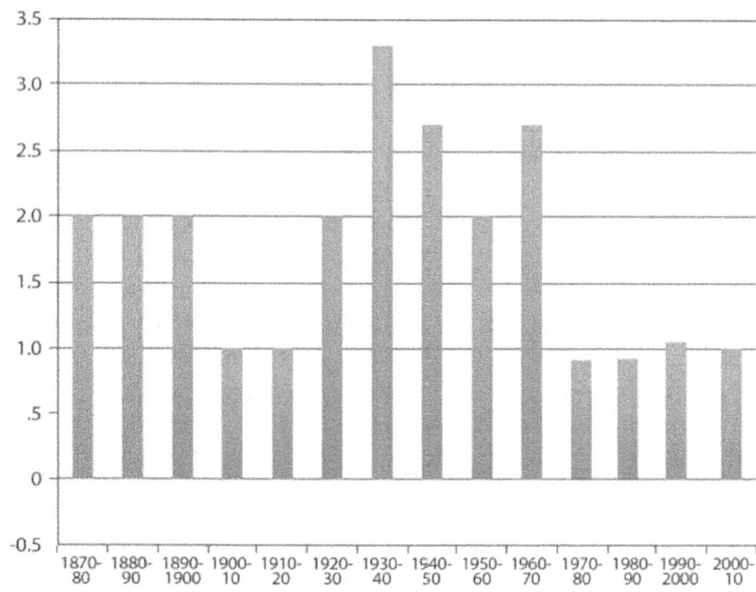

FIGURE 3

Total Factor Productivity in the U.S. Economy

(Annual Growth by Decade)

Source: NBER, Congressional Research Paper "Total Factor Productivity Growth in Historical Perspective", 2013

bending to pressure from something, except from the pressure of the strong presence of Wall Street and of New York real estate billionaires and so forth around this administration, who as I said earlier, are trying to pin the administration to the stock market boom, and the effects of deregulation in industry, the removal of some regulations, especially on small companies—pin it to the idea that that is somehow going to pull the Trump Administration and the U.S. economy through into a big recovery of the kind that Trump wants to cause and has been already talking about.

Remember also that when Lyndon LaRouche got the Strategic Defense Initiative adopted by the Reagan Administration in 1983, the strategic effects of that, and the long-term effects of it were profound all over the world. But, unfortunately, Reagan's people did not go with any greatly improved understanding of LaRouche's economic policies. There were a couple of exceptions in the National Security Council at that time; they were not particularly high-ranking people. Otherwise, if you remember, it was Henry Kissinger's so-called Caribbean Basin Initiative and other things which were the shiny objects that drew the attentions of the principals in the Reagan Administration.

They were doing exactly the right thing strategically, and they had a sense for technology, but they failed to learn economics from LaRouche. Similarly with Tillerson. He thinks that the way in which China is expanding credit now into Belt and Road projects for the development of these other countries is incalculable in terms of what its debt effects will be, and therefore, since we've never done it,—since he's never been associated with any entity private or public that's done it—he doesn't believe it will work.

So I'd say it's a combination of that pressure on the Trump Administration as a whole, and Tillerson's own mindset coming from the industry which, of all industries, has piled the greatest volume of nonproductive, speculative debt on itself in the last 10 years—it's orders of magnitude higher than any other industry, from the smallest shale wildcatters up to the ExxonMobil. And I don't think it is in any way associated in his mind with an anti-China strategic view at all.

Question: You started by describing Wall Street wanting a 10% return on a 10-year bond, to finance infrastructure, but infrastructure would usually take a longer time, 30 years, to produce a result, and in an open economy like the United States as you pointed out, there's tertiary and secondary benefits for the act of constructing a major project; but those benefits don't flow to the party that is doing the infrastructure financing.

On the other hand, the Chinese economy is a closed-loop economy, and to some extent, as they invest in developing countries, they can capture secondary benefits through direct economic activity in the country related to the infrastructure project.

In terms of looking at the cost or the value of an infrastructure project, how could there be devised, other than starting a bank, which is a control feature, how could there be devised, call it a reward, on some basis for the lack of a specific return related to an infrastructure financing? That is a problem I think that maybe would be worth trying to solve.

Gallagher: I would say, this is why Alexander Hamilton, when forming the First National Bank, who was obviously informed directly by the experience and the projects he was involved in, said, in effect, "Bring all your tired, your poor, your nonperforming holders of U.S. debt and colonial debt" to me, and put it in this bank. You're not going to get paid anything on your principal for 20 years, but you're going to get, in most cases, 6+2% annual return. So you're going to put it with us for a long period of time, you're going to get a good return; it's going to be backed by the taxes that we are enacting in order to finance the dividends of this bank."

We can do that again now. All those holders of all that $7.5 trillion of relatively long-term, publicly held U.S. Treasury debt: Bring it here, put it in this bank, for 20 years or more! And capitalize this bank, turn it into equity with a dividend of 4-5%.

It is the crucial method by which we organize the selection of the specific investments that that bank is going to make, the selection of the projects. How we organize the directors and the experience of the directors in order to make sure that it's carried out in the way that Harry Hopkins and Harold Ickes made sure that great infrastructure projects of Roosevelt were not encumbered by graft and incompetence and so forth. That's the key: how are we going to invest it?

Question: [follow-up] The problem with that is municipal bonds are a method of raising infrastructure money and are tax free, tax exempt. That's inducing investors to avoid paying taxes on the income related to those bonds. So that would be similar to your suggestion. In the case of Harry Hopkins, there were no other choices; we were in a Depression. And gluing together a big bank and getting people to march into that, seems unrealistic. So is there a way to do it, on a more indirect basis?

Gallagher: You're obviously recoiling against "big." But we're currently investing, nationally, in infrastructure about $200 billion a year, and that covers everything, from fixing windows on elementary schools, to building new bridges. And the great majority of that is being done by municipalities, by state and local governments, not by the federal government. The federal government is effectively investing nothing.

And against that, we have the demand, the obvious need, for multiple trillions of dollars of investment in infrastructure. We have to do something *big*. This is one way to do it. I'm suggesting that we do it the way that Alexander Hamilton did it, because that's clearly one way to do it that worked. That's why we're suggesting, do it that way.

But there is going to be plenty of return for the companies that carry out these projects and for the local

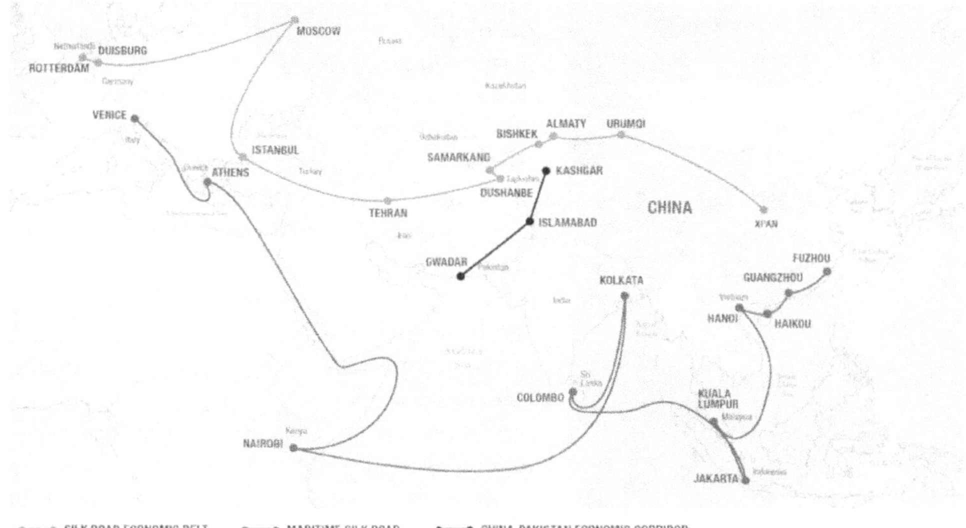

banks which make loans to those companies which are carrying out the projects—

Question: [follow-up] Those are secondary and tertiary returns.

Gallagher: Sure!

Question: [follow-up] Not to the direct provider of the money.

Gallagher: Yes, because, like the Reconstruction Finance Corp., as the final report of the RFC said when they wrapped it up in '56, it wasn't intended to make a profit, but over the long term it did. *But that was not its purpose.* Its purpose was to carry out the national purposes of the United States, and that was a big thing: It was $55 billion worth of credit at that time, of lending over that period of time. For that time it was very big. It operated as a lending institution overwhelmingly, and really, in a certain way as a commercial bank, and that's exactly how our Hamiltonian bank should operate, as a commercial bank. It's got to be big, and it's going to make it possible for things to get done that are going to raise the productivity of everybody participating, and therefore, raise the profitability of a lot of the corporations and local banks that participate. It's going to discount their loans; it's going to buy the infrastructure bonds of municipalities that are newly issued. That's what I'd say.

We have to look at it in a different way: China has set loose upon the world, an offer, and as I mentioned earlier, this wasn't even seen as the right thing to do, or an important thing to do, by many economists and officials in China when Xi Jinping first started the Belt and Road. Now it appears they do. China has put before the world an offer of exactly the kind of investment that I was just discussing with the previous questioner—that it is willing to make these kinds of investments over long periods of time,—what they call "patient capital"—they're going to wait a long time. We don't have that definition in America of "patient capital," but in China they do; it's a very rigorous definition that they use. They're willing to make capital available, for the most important productivity enhancing projects in any country, obviously with a certain rough, overall design, that started out, as Helga and Lyn did, with the land-bridges across the Eurasian continent; but nonetheless, this is a matter of increasing the productivity and decreasing the poverty in countries all over the world. They have that offer out there.

It's not geopolitical. It doesn't involve saying, "I want you on my side in a war against so-and-so." No matter how inconceivable they may think that war is, they're not saying to any country, "I want you on my side in this war." They are very much under pressure right now by the North Korean crisis. They definitely do *not* want war there, and they definitely do not want the collapse of the North Korean regime either, because of what that will cause. They're in a very difficult spot to pursue their policy, what Helga calls the "Confucian policy" of mutual benefit. They're trying to do it.

I don't think by any means that Trump gets that, in any full sense, but the fact that there are mutual benefits to be had, he can see that. That's why I really think we could see something happening on this trip to Asia; it's really up to us, what we do.

LaRouche versus Rohatyn

Moderator Dennis Speed: I'd like to point something out, because a lot of people do not know it, which

Glass-Steagall opponent Felix Rohatyn—here is Washington, D.C., March 27, 2006—makes up for his incompetence by advocating productivity-destroying austerity.

is that in 1974-75, Paul was the leader of our New York organization, the National Committee member in this area. And we had a legendary fight, or it should be legendary, with Felix Rohatyn at that time, when the Municipal Assistance Corporation, or Big MAC, was imposed on the City of New York.

Paul had an exchange back at that time, or we had an exchange, with David Rockefeller, who was no great fan of ours, and I was caused to think about it, as we were getting some of the questions, because underlying many of the questions is that there are two worldviews on the question of the nature of economy and the nature of man.

Gallagher: I had a more recent exchange with Felix Rohatyn, ten years ago at a conference in a big think tank in Washington, where a number of us were intervening, and there were a number of Congressmen speaking, and Rohatyn was there. And at certain point, I got the floor, and brought up Franklin Roosevelt's methods of investing in infrastructure and the New Deal, developing the productivity of the economy in the New Deal. Rohatyn reacted, and simply said, "We don't need Roosevelt. No. We do not any longer need Roosevelt. We now have deep private markets,. . ." and so on. He went on, "We don't need to use any methods of Franklin Roosevelt."

Rohatyn has been identified for 40 years with pub-

lic-private partnerships and with so-called infrastructure banks based on public-private partnerships. That's been shown now, over that entire period of time, to be a failing strategy, a failing practice; and not only in the United States, but also there are recent reports of some spectacular failures in private attempts to rebuild the Autobahn between Hamburg and Dortmund in Germany.

This fleecing has happened time and time and time again, with so-called privately built infrastructure, or public-private partnership infrastructure here; so that when we put out the report last year, "Hamilton not Rohatyn," we were really talking about not only a method that worked as opposed to a method that doesn't work; at the same time, we were talking about a view of the human being where a country grows and develops wealth on the basis of its own productive capacities, on the basis of its own inventions, and the expansion of its own productive capacities, and only trades secondarily.

Our view is that the human being is inherently inventive. Look at Jason Ross' and Ben Deniston's class from this past Wednesday night, and particularly the quotations that John Sigerson read from Abraham Lincoln about the unique, inventive quality of the human being, and how it expresses itself in an economy. That came from Hamilton: Lincoln was a devoted Hamiltonian; he had the same policy and the same view of the inventiveness, the capacity for discovery and increased productivity of the human species, coming from the inventiveness of the individual human being.

The British System is the opposite: That the wealth of the country comes from its trade, from producing a few things and selling them, and its ability to develop financial services. That's Rohatyn's view of it, that the United States is a leader, because it has such deep financial service capabilities in order to make these new infrastructure projects possible all over the world. But it just hasn't happened, it doesn't happen. Because what they want out of this is financiers' profits.

What we're demanding in LaRouche's laws is a massive investment in the productivity of the economy, which does not involve profits for financiers. It involves the productivity of the people who build it.

Originally published in EIR,

August 11, 1995

Non-Newtonian Mathematics For Economists

by Lyndon H. LaRouche, Jr.

The following economic advisory should be read as a sequel to the feature, "Why Most Nobel Prize Economists Are Quacks," EIR, July 28, 1995 [republished in EIR, Oct. 27, 2017]. In that feature, the author referenced the reader to his relevant work on the issues of mathematical representation of the cause-effect relations characteristic of real economic processes. In the following EIR Special Economics Feature, he summarizes the method to be employed.

The onrushing process of collapse of the International Monetary Fund-dominated global monetary and financial system, demonstrates, among other points, that all generally accepted mathematical representations of economic processes are devastatingly incompetent. The relevant alternative is named the LaRouche-Riemann method. However, a world which has suffered so much under the policies of the U.S. Nobel Prize-winners, should not be asked to accept an alternative economic teaching on blind faith. Therefore, it is not sufficient to know that the LaRouche-Riemann method works; it is necessary to render transparent both how, and why it works.

Two problems must be addressed, in selecting a method of measurement for representing real economic processes. The primary task is to define a method for representing the physical-economic process as such: This process is characteristically "not-entropic."[1] The

secondary, but also crucial task, is that of representing the interaction between that economic process and a superimposed, characteristically linear (and, therefore entropic) monetary and financial system.

The method required for representing the real economy, the physical-economic process, is described, step-by-step, as follows.

LaRouche's Discovery

The discovery upon which that LaRouche-Riemann method is based, was initially developed during the interval 1948-52. It originated in a commitment to a narrower purpose, that of showing the absurdity of Prof. Norbert Wiener's insistence that the communication of human conceptions could be measured in the terms of his statistical "information theory."[2] The decision to use

---

1. On the subject of the present writer's use of the term "not-entropy." It has been widely accepted classroom doctrine, for more than a century, that all inorganic processes tend to run down; this argument was posed by Britain's Lord Kelvin, during the middle of the last century. On Kelvin's instruction, his doctrine was given a mathematical form by two German academics, Rudolf Clausius and Hermann Grassman, who employed their own kinematic model of heat-exchange, in an imaginary, confined, particular gas-system, as a purported explanation of French

scientist Sadi Carnot's caloric theory of heat. Kelvin and his collaborators defined the "frictional" loss of extractable work in such a mechanical model of a thermodynamical system, as "entropy." This was Kelvin's Second Law of Thermodynamics. During the 1940s, the Massachusetts Institute of Technology's Prof. Norbert Wiener employed the term "negative entropy" (shortened to the neologism "negentropy") to signify the statistical form of "reversed entropy," in the sense of a famous reconstruction of the Clausius-Grassman model by Ludwig Boltzmann: Boltzmann's so-called H-theorem. Wiener's argument was employed to found what has become known as "information theory." In this connection, Wiener claimed that the H-theorem provided a statistical means for measuring the "information content" of not only coded electronic transmissions, but also human communication of ideas. Earlier usage had identified "negative entropy" as a characteristic of the apparent violation of Kelvin's so-called "Second Law" by living processes in general, as distinct from the ostensibly entropic characteristics of ordinary non-living phenomena. For several decades, beginning 1948, this writer insisted that only the first meaning of "negentropy," as typified by the commonly characteristic distinction of living processes, should be accepted usage. Recently, for practical reasons, he has substituted the term "not-entropy."

2. Norbert Wiener, *Cybernetics* (New York: John Wiley & Sons, 1948).

Mathematician Carl Friedrich Gauss, the chief patron of Bernhard Riemann. Contrary to the Newtonians, the faction of Gauss and Riemann was committed to the idea that the universe is ruled by an efficient principle of Reason.

the facts of physical economy for this refutation of Wiener, led to the discovery.

That original argument deployed against Wiener's presumption, was that human "ecology" differs from that of lower species in the same general sense, that living processes differ characteristically from what we regard conventionally as non-living processes. This argument was premised on the fact, that the increase of the *potential relative population-density*[3] of the human

species, through such means as technological progress, represented a succession of clearly distinguishable phase-shifts: that these characteristic phase-shifts in the development of society, distinguish the human species absolutely from all lower species.

The initial representation of this distinction between mankind and the inferior species, was elementary: the standpoint of geometry. Any logically consistent form of mathematical mapping of an existing range of technology can be described, with effective approximation, in the form of a deductive theorem-lattice. Any valid discovery of a superior principle, has the effect upon mathematical physics, for example, of requiring a corresponding change in the set of formal and ontological axioms underlying the pre-existing, generally accepted form of mathematical physics. It is the cumulative succession of such efficiently progressive, axiomatic changes in human knowledge for practice, which corresponds to the succession of phase-shifts in range of society's potential relative population-density.

This view defined an implied, functional ordering-principle underlying the increase of potential relative population-density. The initial thesis of the 1948-54 interval was, summarily, as follows. Let the physical and related consumption by households and the productive cycle, be regarded as analogous to the use of the term "energy of the system" in undergraduate thermodynamics. Societies rise or fall, in the degree to which they not only meet that "energy of the system" requirement, but also generate a margin of increased output of those qualities of requirement, which is analogous to "free energy." We have thus, implicitly, a ratio of "free energy" to "energy of the system."

An additional consideration is crucial. The development of society requires that a significant portion of that "free energy" be "re-invested" in the form of "energy of

---

As of 1948, there existed two principal, previously developed premises in this writer's knowledge, for his competence to assault Wiener's thesis. During the late 1930s, this writer, already a dedicated follower of Gottfried Leibniz, had been deeply involved in constructing a proof of the absurdity of the arguments against Leibniz central to Immanuel Kant's *Critique of Pure Reason.* In 1948, he recognized the crucial fallacies of Wiener's "statistical information theory" to be a crude replication of the central argument, on the subject of the theory of knowledge, in Kant's three famous *Critiques.* Secondly, by 1946-47, the writer's interest had become absorbed with his own somewhat critical view of the use of the notion of "negative entropy" in biology, as, for example, by LeComte du Nouy.

3. Lyndon H. LaRouche, Jr., *So, You Wish To Learn All About Economics?* (New York: New Benjamin Franklin House, 1984), *passim.* "Relative" in "potential relative population-density" signifies, simply, the differences in quality of man-developed, and man-depleted habitat referenced.

the system." This must not merely expand the scale of the society; it must increase the relative "capital-intensity" and "energy-intensity" of society's production, per capita and per unit of land-area employed. Thus, some minimal value of the ratio of "free energy" to "energy of the system" must be sustained, despite rising "capital-intensity" and "energy-intensity" of the mode used for the productive cycle. This constraint (array of inequalities) was employed to define the proper use of the term "negentropy," in counterposition to Wiener's use of the term. Recently, the term "not-entropy" was adopted as better serving this purpose.

About 1949-50, the argument against Wiener assumed this form. Since the characteristic distinction of the human species is the series of phase-shifts in potential relative population-density, describable in this way: The *ideas* which are characteristic of the successful thinking of cultures, are those ideas represented efficiently as the changes in practice which tend to increase the potential relative population-density of the human species. It is this implicit social content of each valid axiomatic-revolutionary discovery in science or art, which defines human knowledge: not Wiener's mechanistic, statistical approach.

It was already apparent, at that point in the investigation, that no conventional classroom mathematics was adequate for mapping this kind of "not-entropic" economic process. The central function of valid axiomatic-revolutionary ideas, locates the function of economic growth in the revolutionary changes in axioms as such. The mathematical problem so presented, is that changes in the sets of axioms underlying deductive theorem-lattices, have the form of *absolute mathematical discontinuities*. That is: There is no formal method for reaching the new lattice deductively from the old. Such a mathematical discontinuity has a magnitude of unlimited smallness never reaching actual zero. That implies the existence of very powerful, extremely useful sorts of mathematical functions, but no ordinary notion of mathematics can cope with functions which are expressed in terms of such discontinuities. To apply the writer's original discovery, this problem of mathematical representation had to be addressed next. *A mathematical solution would be desirable, but a conceptual overview was indispensable.*

Thus, the next step, in early 1952, proved to be a study of Georg Cantor's treatment of those kinds of mathematical discontinuities.[4] The study of Cantor's

work on the subject of the mathematically transfinite, especially his so-called Aleph-series, pointed toward access to a deeper appreciation of the 1854 habilitation dissertation of Bernhard Riemann. Conversely, Riemann's fundamental discovery respecting the generalization of "non-Euclidean" geometries, showed how we must think of Cantor's functional notion of *implicitly enumerable density of mathematical discontinuities per arbitrarily chosen interval of action.*

That notion of relative density of discontinuities is the proper description of the culture which society transmits to its young.[5] This notion of "density," references the accumulation of those valid scientific and artistic discoveries of principle (e.g., valid axiomatic-revolutionary changes), which mankind to date has accumulated to transmit to the educational experience of the young individuals.

Once one recognizes that Cantor's work is retracing the discovery made earlier by Riemann, there is an obvious advantage of choosing Riemann's geometrical approach, over the relatively formalistic route used by Cantor.[6] In the design of productive and related processes in modern economy, the conceptions which un-

---

lehre, Georg Cantor: Gesammelte Abhandlungen mathematischen und philosophischen Inhalts, Ernst Zermelo, ed. (1932) (Berlin: Verlag von Julius Springer, 1990), pp. 282-356. The standard English translation of this work, by the Franco-English critic of Cantor, Philip E.B. Jourdain, is published as Georg Cantor, *Contributions to the Founding of the Theory of Transfinite Numbers* (New York: Dover Publications, Inc., 1955). The publisher's note for the current reprint edition implies, erroneously, that Dover first published this in 1956. The author's original copy of the Dover reprint of the Jourdain translation (still in the writer's possession) was purchased, in a Minneapolis, Minnesota bookstore, in 1952. Caution is suggested in reading Jourdain's Preface and lengthy Introduction to this translation; in real life, that translator was not quite the faithful collaborator of Cantor which he pretends to have been.
5. Or, one might say, relative *cardinality* or *power.*
6. As a result of the control of the Berlin Academy of Science by the Newton devotee Frederick II of Prussia, and the subsequent, post-1814 takeover of France's Ecole Polytechnique by the Newtonians Laplace and Cauchy, the geometric method of Plato, Cusa, Leonardo da Vinci, Kepler, and Leibniz tended to be supplanted by the method of algebraic infinite series. Most significant was Leonhard Euler's attack upon Leibniz, on the issue of infinite algebraic series: Euler's denial of the existence of absolute mathematical discontinuities. The political success of the Newtonians, over the course of the Nineteenth Century, in establishing Euler's infinite series for natural logarithms as a standard of mathematical proof, led into the positivism of the Russell-Whitehead *Principia Mathematica,* and the, related, wild-eyed extremism of present-day "chaos theory." Thus, Karl Weierstrass and his former pupil, Georg Cantor, while attacking the same general problem of mathematics as Riemann, the existence of discontinuities, engaged the Newtonian adversary on his own terrain, infinite series, whereas Riemann attacked the problem from the standpoint of geometry: hence, Riemann's notably greater success for physics.

---

4. Georg Cantor, *Beiträge zur Begründung der transfiniten Mengen-*

derlie the design of scientific experiments, and of derived machine-tool conceptions, are intrinsically geometric in nature. To think about production and economy, one must think geometrically, not algebraically.

Hence, the present writer's use of Riemann's work to address the mathematical implications of his own earlier discovery in economics, acquired the seemingly anomalous, but precisely descriptive name of the "LaRouche-Riemann Method."[7] Examine the most elementary of the relevant features of Riemann's habilitation dissertation.[8] For for the purpose of clarity, the following passages repeat several of the points stated immediately above.

In the conclusion of his famous, 1854 habilitation dissertation, "On the Hypotheses Which Underlie Geometry," Riemann summarizes his argument: "This leads us to the domain of another science, into the realm of physics, which the nature of today's occasion [i.e., mathematics—LHL] does not permit us to enter."[9] In

present-day classroom terms, that statement of Riemann's has the following principal implications bearing upon the construction of a mathematical schema capable of adequately representing real economic processes.

Any *deductive* system of mathematics can be described as a formal theorem-lattice. A *theorem* in such a lattice is any proposition which is proven to be not inconsistent with an underlying set of interconnected *axioms and postulates*.[10] The relevant model of reference for this notion of a theorem-lattice, is either a Euclidean geometry, or, preferably, the constructive type of geometry associated with the famous names of Gaspard Monge, Adrien M. Legendre, and Bernhard Riemann's geometry instructor, Jacob Steiner.

This presents the difficulty, that any alteration within that set of axioms and postulates, generates a new theorem-lattice, which is pervasively inconsistent with the first. This inconsistency between the two, is expressed otherwise as a *mathematical discontinuity,* or a *singularity.* When defined in this proper way, to show the existence of such a discontinuity signifies, that no theorem of the second theorem-lattice can be directly accessed from the starting-point of the first, unless we introduce the notion of the operation responsible for the relevant change within the set of axioms.

In other words, we must depart *pre-existing* mathematics, and detour, by way of *physics as such,* to reach the second of the two mathematical theorem-lattices. The crucial term of reference which we must introduce at this juncture, as Nicolaus of Cusa prescribed in his work founding modern science,[11] as Riemann does, is "measurement."[12] Consider this writer's favorite, frequently referenced classroom illustration of the principle involved.

Consider the estimation of the size of the Earth's polar meridian, by the famous member of Plato's Academy of Athens, Eratosthenes; a measurement of the curvature of the Earth made during the third century B.C., twenty-two centuries before any man was to have seen the curvature of the Earth.[13] The twofold point to be

---

7. Although this writer consistently referenced this debt to Riemann during his one-semester course taught at various campuses during the 1966-73 interval, the first published use of the term "LaRouche-Riemann" method originated in November 1978, when the term was adopted for the purposes of a joint forecasting venture undertaken by the *Executive Intelligence Review,* in cooperation with the Fusion Energy Foundation. At that time, the prompting consideration was the fact that isentropic compression in thermonuclear fusion, as predefined mathematically by Riemann's 1859 *Über die Fortpflanzung ebener Luftwellen von endlicher Schwingungsweite,* has mathematical analogies to the propagation of the "shock-wave"-like phase-shifts generated through technological revolutions. (See, Riemann, *Werke,* pp. 157-175.) As a by-product of this same, highly successful, forecasting project, a translation of the Riemann paper was prepared by the same task-force; this appeared in *The International Journal of Fusion Energy,* Vol. 2, No. 3, 1980, pp. 1-23, under the title, "On the Propagation of Plane Airwaves of Finite Amplitude." This emphasis on Riemann's "shock-wave" paper, reflected an ongoing, friendly quarrel of the period, between the writer's organization and Lawrence Livermore Laboratories, on the mathematics of thermonuclear ignition in inertial confinement. Notably, that conflict reflected the influence of the U.S. Army Air Corps' Anglophile science adviser, Theodore von Karman, in promoting Lord Rayleigh's fanatical incompetency against Riemann's method. On the success of the 1979-83 *EIR Quarterly Economic Forecasts,* see David P. Goldman, "Volcker Caught in Mammoth Fraud," *EIR,* Nov. 1, 1983.
8. Bernhard Riemann, *Über die Hypothesen, welche der Geometrie zu Grunde liegen, Bernhard Riemanns gesammelte mathematische Werke* [hereinafter referenced as "Riemann, *Werke*"], Heinrich Weber, ed. (New York: Dover Publications, Inc. [reprint], 1953), pp. 272-287. Those concerned with the formal-mathematical implications of the dissertation as such, are referred to the later (1858) Paris representation of this: *Commenetatio mathematica, qua respondere tenatur questionii ab IIIma Academia Parisiensi propositae, Werke,* pp. 391-404 (in Latin), with appended notes by Weber: pp. 405-423 (in German).
9. "Es führt dies hinüber in das Gebiet einer andern Wissenschaft, in das Gebiet der Physik, welches wohl die Natur der heutigen Veranlas-

sung nicht zu betreten erlaubt." Loc. cit., p. 286.
10. Plato's term for the set of axioms and postulates underlying a theorem-lattice is *hypothesis.*
11. *De docta ignorantia* (1440), *passim.*
12. Riemann, op. cit., *"II. Ma×verhaeltnisse, deren eine Mannigfaltigkeit von n Dimensionen fähig ist...,"* pp. 276-283.
13. See *Greek Mathematical Works,* Ivor Thomas, trans., Vol. II (Cambridge, Mass.: Harvard University Press, 1980), pp. 266-273. Cf.

Eratosthenes' Measurement of the Size of the Earth

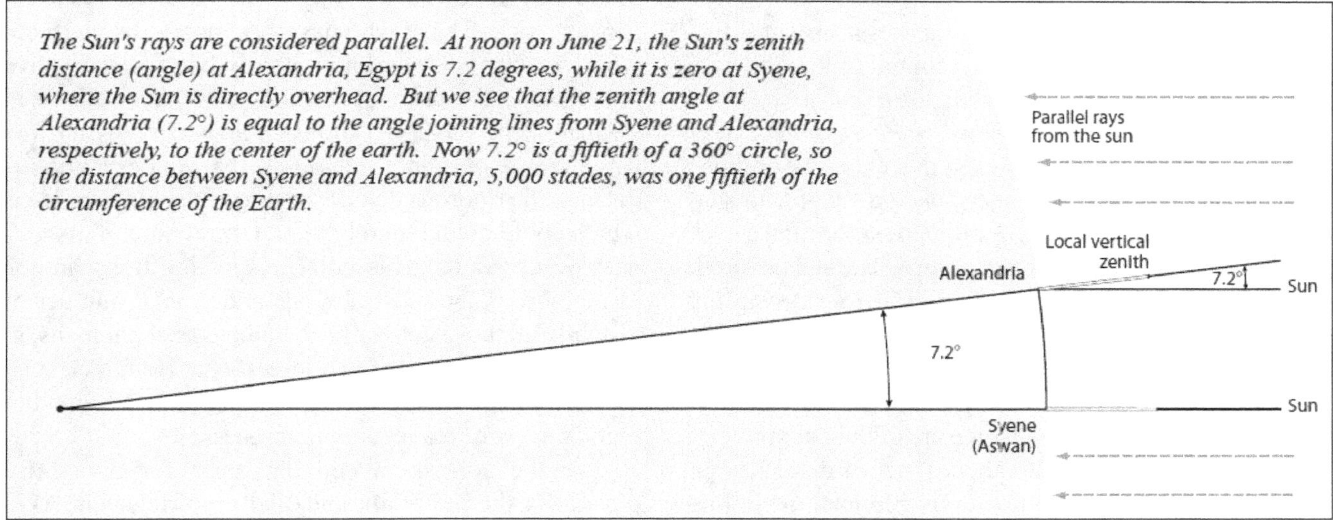

made, is, briefly, as follows.

Using astronomy to determine a North-South line (a meridian of longitude), choose two points of significant, but measurable distance along that line, between them. Measure that distance. Construct identical sundials at each of the two points. Measure the shadow which a vertical stick casts, at noon on the same day, and compare the angles of the respective shadows. The difference between the two angles is adumbrated by the fact, that the Earth is not flat, but has a definite curvature (see **Figure 1**). Using the geometric principle of similarity and proportion, estimate the size of the circle passing through the Earth's two poles on the basis of the measured length of the arc-distance between the two points. Eratosthenes was off by about fifty miles, in estimating the polar diameter of the Earth.[14]

The two points illustrated by this example, are as follows.

First, this example illustrates what Plato signifies by an *idea.* Since this measurement was made twenty-two centuries before anyone had seen the curvature of the Earth, what was measured was not an object defined by sense-perception. The senses were employed, of course; but, the idea of curvature was derived from the certainty that the evidence of the senses was self-contradictory:

The difference in the angles of the shadow at the two points was the empirical expression of that self-contradictory quality. It was necessary to go to conceptions which existed outside the scope of sense-perceptions: into the realm which Plato defines as that of ideas.[15]

Second, this, like related ancient Greek discoveries, leads into the modern geodesy developed by Riemann's chief patron, Carl F. Gauss: the measurement of distances along the surface of the Earth, under the control of reference to astronomical measurements.[16]

Some reader might be tempted to object: "Why not

Lyndon H. LaRouche, Jr., "What Is God, That Man Is In His Image?," *Fidelio,* Spring 1995, pp. 28-29.
14. Ibid.

---

15. Divide the domain of science as a whole among three topical areas, areas differentiated from one another by the limitations of man's powers of sense-perception. Let what can be identified as a phenomenon, by the sense-perceptual apparatus, be named the domain of *macrophysics.* What is inaccessible in the very large (such as seeing directly the phenomenon of the distance between the Earth and the Moon), belongs to the domain of *astrophysics.* Phenomena which occur on a scale too small for discrimination directly by our senses, are of the domain of *microphysics.* Thus, the most elementary physical ideas of astrophysics and microphysics belong entirely to the domain of Platonic ideas. It is the student's practice of rigor in reliving the discoveries of Plato's Academy at Athens, and of Archimedes, from the Fourth and Third Centuries, B.C., which is the prerequisite training of the student's powers of judgment, for addressing the domains of astrophysics and microphysics. More fundamental, is what might be set aside, for purposes of classroom discussion, as a fourth department of scientific events: *causality.* The senses could never show us the *cause* of even those events which sense-perception might adequately identify: Cause exists for knowledge only in the domain of Platonic ideas.
16. See *C.F. Gauss: Werke,* Vol. IX (New York: Georg Olms Verlag, 1981), *passim.*

say simply 'trigonometry'; why use the term which is probably stranger to the layman, 'geodesy'?" The critic would be committing a serious error, a type of error which is of direct relevance to the point at hand. Expressed as a recipe, the relevant rebuttal of the criticism is: *We should always state what we claim to know in terms of the manner in which we came to know it.* It is through recognizing, Socratically, that either we or those who taught us, might have overlooked a significant step of judgment actually taken, or omitted, in forming a conception, that crucial errors of assumption are uncovered, and corrected. More broadly, it is by reconsidering the way in which we acquired conceptions, by taking that process as an object of epistemological scrutiny, that a true scientific rigor is cultivated. In layman's terms: that we might come to know what we are talking about.

We should define Eratosthenes' act of discovery in the manner we might competently replicate it. It was through astronomy that Eratosthenes estimated the polar circumference of the Earth. He did this by methods which are related to the earlier proof, by Aristarchus, that the Earth orbited the Sun, and, also, the methods by which Eratosthenes estimated the distance of the Moon from the Earth, the latter a distance which no man was to have seen until about twenty-two-hundred years later. That is what we know in this matter; it should never be reformulated in a different fashion.

It is violations of our methodological prescription here, which are key to the way in which Isaac Newton, for example, stumbled into his fraudulent *et hypotheses non fingo,* and that numerous other frauds of Newton and his devotees were generated, and credulously adopted by later generations of students. As Riemann emphasized, contrary to Newton's somewhat hysterical insistence that he made no hypotheses, Newton made a very obvious hypothetical assumption, on which his mathematical physics depends entirely. Riemann identified one aspect of that error;[17] but one may apply the same method used by Riemann there, to show that the entirety of the Newtonian system, in the present-day classroom, rests upon that same fallacious hypothesis. Had Newton, or his followers, paid closer attention to the method by which the Newtonians actually reached the opinions which they claimed as their knowledge, they probably would not have dared continue such blunders, nor chant their ritual *hypotheses non fingo.*

Those who profess to know the answer because they looked it up in the back of the textbook, or because someone has told them, have merely "learned" that sort of answer, somewhat as a dog might have learned to retrieve a stick. Those who have not merely learned, but who *know* the answer, know it only because they have either made the original discovery, or have relived it, step by step. What we *know—knowledge—*is not the fruit of sense-certainty, but, rather, that which came to us through the rigorous demonstration of the kinds of ideas which could not be merely the interpretation of eyewitness observations. This point, respecting transparency of method, is the most obvious and crucial blunder of virtually all those generally accredited as economists, to date, who have claimed to address what is, in fact, such an ontologically complex subject-matter as the mathematical view of real economic processes.

For the competent economist, as for thoughtful physicists, the essential fraud of all empiricism, is: Akin to the traditional Aristoteleanism from which it is derived, empiricism insists that it addresses only the measurement of observed phenomena, free of the assumption of any governing hypothesis. This fraud is typified by Newton's *et hypotheses non fingo.* Contrary to that fraud, the indispensable role of the continuing improvement of formal mathematics as such, is to provide more powerful instruments of analysis for testing the consistency of any given formal theorem-lattice. Economy of effort in science requires, that we be able to expose, more directly and quickly, the nature of inconsistency between the axiomatic basis underlying a theorem-lattice and some given, empiricist or other, presumption respecting how we ought to measure.[18] Eratosthenes' referenced measurement of the meridian is a simple illustration of that principle of science: the principle of scientific, i.e., Platonic, ideas.

In mathematics, or mathematical physics, such a Platonic form of idea is exemplified by the form of a set of axioms underlying any formal system, as what Plato and Riemann recognize as *hypothesis.* When we are speaking of formal theorem-lattice systems, such as a formal mathematics, "hypothesis" signifies the set of axiomatic assumptions underlying all provable theorems of a particular type of theorem-lattice (such as a Euclidean geometry, a linear algebra, etc.).[19]

---

17. Riemann, *Werke,* p. 525.

18. Such an inconsistency does not prove, intrinsically, either that the proposition, or the mathematics is wrong. It forces us to conceptualize the idea of the existence of such an inconsistency.

19. In short, when a speaker employs the term "hypothesis" as a synonym for "conjectured," or "intuited" solution to a riddle, for example,

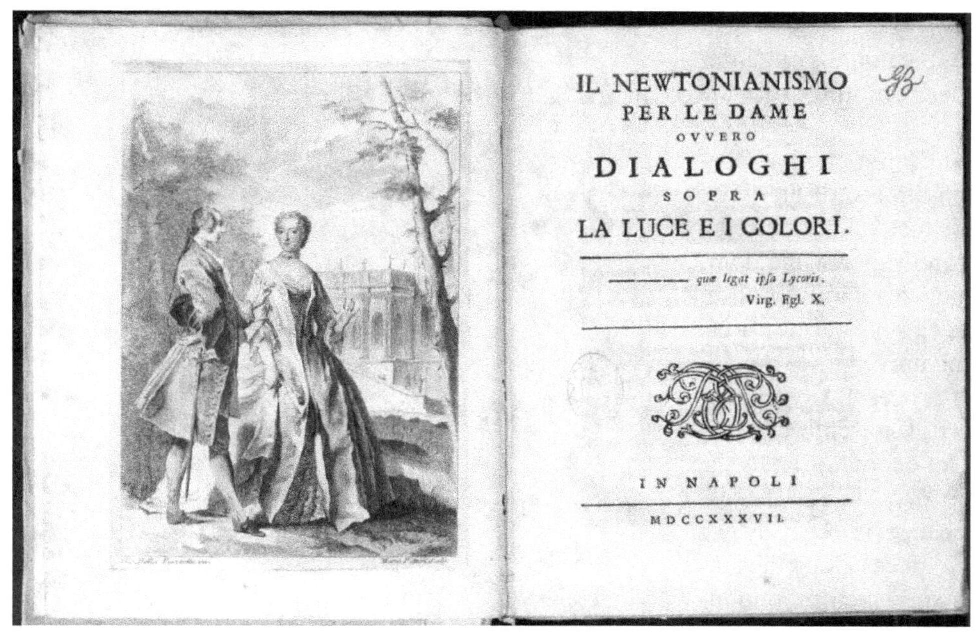

Building the cult of Isaac Newton: Venetian author Francesco Algorotti's 1737 "Newtonianism for the Lady."

The pupil who had received a good secondary education, a Classical humanist form of such education, would already have mastered some of the precedents for this: 1) He would be familiar, from the work of Plato's Academy at Athens, and Archimedes, with the distinction between systems of mathematics limited to "commensurables," and the so-called "incommensurables." 2) He would know Nicolaus of Cusa's conclusive proof of the division of the domain of the "incommensurables," between what we term the "irrationals" and the "transcendentals." 3) In his introductory education in the calculus, that student would also have come to understand how Leibniz and Jean Bernoulli showed the incompetence of Descartes' and Newton's "algebraic methods" (e.g., "infinite series"), and why, from the standpoint of the physics of refraction of light, "algebraic" methods must be replaced by "non-algebraic," or "transcendental" notions of mathematical function. 4) He might also know, that the emergence of the notion of the Riemann Surface function and Cantor's Aleph series, is traceable from those notions of mathematical

discontinuities central to the mathematical work of Cusa and Leibniz's articulation of a differential calculus, the notion of discontinuities hysterically denied by Newton devotee Leonhard Euler.

In each historical case, such as the subsumption of all notions of magnitude under the generalization of "incommensurables," mathematics undergoes an axiomatic change within its underlying assumptions, its *hypothesis*. So, by the proof, cued to Ole Rømer's crucial measurement of the speed of light, of the experimentally demonstrable nature of generalized refraction of light, Leibniz and Bernoulli established the domain of the transcendental, as earlier demanded by Nicolaus of Cusa, who introduced the *isoperimetric principle,*[20] this the axiomatic basis for the mathematics of the transcendental domain. The linear hypothesis of Euclidean space-time (axiomatic self-evidence of points and lines), was superseded by the principle of the cycloid: a space-time in which (Cusa's) isoperimetricism, least time, and least action govern in a unified way.[21] The Riemann Surface function, and Cantor's Aleph-series, implicitly define a physical universe in which the existence of not-entropic (e.g., living and cognitive) processes is not merely permitted, but necessary. Riemann's habilitation dissertation, his work on the Riemann Surface, upon plane air waves, and so on, all

---

the speaker is showing himself to be illiterate in science. However, that sort of illiteracy does not identify the precise sense in which Isaac Newton misuses the same term; Newton's argument is that of the radical philosophical empiricists in the tradition of Sarpi, Galileo, Hobbes, Descartes, et al.: Newton is asserting that he relies solely upon sense-certainty. Newton is insisting—however wrongly—that there are nothing but "natural ingredients" of sense-phenomena in his system.

20. Op. cit., *passim.* Cusa reworked Archimedes' theorems on quadrature of the circle, producing what he identified as a superior approach to Archimedes' determination of *pi*. This discovery was incorporated in *De docta ignorantia* (1440), but supplied a formal elaboration in his "On the Quadrature of the Circle," (1450) W. Wertz, trans., *Fidelio,* Spring 1994, pp. 56-63. The new principle of hypothesis, which Cusa develops on the basis of his proof that *pi* is transcendental, is known as the isoperimetric principle: The Euclid axioms, that point and straight line are self-evident, are discarded, and replaced by that isoperimetric principle which, in first approximation, treats the existence of circular action as primary (e.g., "self-evident").

21. See "20. John and Jacob Bernouilli, The Brachystochrone," *A Source Book in Mathematics 1200-1800,* D.J. Struik, ed., (Princeton, N.J.: Princeton University Press, 1986), pp. 391-399.

address this historical evolution of the notions of geometry under the impact of those ideas erupting from the domain of physics.

For the economist, the crucial point is, that economic processes exist only within the last of the types of geometry we have just listed: that of not-entropic processes, of the process of mankind's increasing domination of the universe: per capita, per family household, and per relevant unit of the Earth's surface area. That domination signifies, that the universe we are addressing is, itself, a not-entropic process. Any mathematics not appropriate to this sort of not-entropic process, is intrinsically incompetent for economic analysis.

Eratosthenes' referenced discovery, like related discoveries, implies a qualitative change in the way we should think about measuring differences along the surface of the Earth, and also the way in which astronomical observations are read. The corroborating differences in measurement to which we are led, axiomatically, by those ideas, posed in that way, reflect the *efficiency* of such a discovery: the proof of any axiomatic-revolutionary, or related discovery, is not its apparent formal consistency with an existing mathematics, but, rather, that it increases the human species' power in the universe.

The referenced examples of changes in types of mathematics, illustrate the point. As illustrated by the Eratosthenes case, once that type of proof of an idea is obtained, we must then modify the axioms of geometry to such effect that we have constructed a new mathematics, a new theorem-lattice. This step takes us into the midst of the discovery which Riemann presents in his habilitation dissertation.

Riemann's Discovery

It must be emphasized here, that the opening two paragraphs of Riemann's habilitation dissertation, which are subtitled "Plan of the Investigation," represent an utterance ranking, for its pungency, force, and direction, in the front rank among all scientific statements ever made.[22] That pungency reflects the fact, that this is one of the most fundamental discoveries in the history of science as a whole. That quality, which permeates the dissertation, demands that the work be read and studied with a clear head, as few putative authorities appear to have done, to the present date: even including the Albert Einstein who praised the work.[23] We

------

22. *"Plan der Untersuchung,"* Riemann, *Werke*, pp. 272-273.

23. Despite the early influence of Ernst Mach's positivism, Einstein

Another view of Isaac Newton: Harpo Marx in the 1957 Hollywood film "The Story of Mankind."

now summarize the crucial implications of Riemann's discovery for economics, restating the case in the terms of the writer's own thesis.

Mathematics, all geometry included, is not a product of the senses, but of the imagination. In the principal part, our mathematics are rooted within the ideas of geometry; what most persons, including professional devotees of the Galileo-Newton tradition, consider mathe-

------

repeatedly showed himself a moral, as well as most capable scientist. His acknowledgement of the debt to Bernhard Riemann's habilitation dissertation, as to Johannes Kepler, like his later collaboration with Kurt Gödel, typifies this. There is a consistent quality to these expressions of his morality in science; Einstein's expression of disgust with the fraudulent physics adopted by the 1920s Solvay Conferences, "God does not play dice," illustrates this. This morality centers around a consistent commitment to the rule of the universe by some efficient principle of Reason, in the sense that Plato, Nicolaus of Cusa, Kepler, Leibniz, Gauss, and Riemann are committed to that principle of science. However, as in his qualified defense of Max Planck, against the savagery of Mach's fanatically positivist devotees, he halts at the point the issue demands a thorough-going repudiation of the essential assumptions of empiricism.

matics, is derived from a naive conception of simple Euclidean solid geometry. Now focus upon a more narrowly defined aspect of the general problem so posed: the fallacies inhering in the attempt to construct mathematical economic models on the basis of a Newtonian form of today's generally accepted university-classroom mathematics.

That mathematics is derived from a special view of a conjectured Euclidean model for space-time. That space is assumed to be ontologically an empty space, defined by three senses of perfectly continuous, limitless extension: up-down, side-to-side, and backward-forward. This space is situated within a notion of time, as also

Bernhard Riemann: The opening paragraphs of his habilitation dissertation stand in the front rank among all scientific statements ever made.

perfectly continuous extension, in but one sense of direction: backward-forward. This can be identified usefully as a notion of geometry derived from the naive imagination. Those four senses of perfectly continuous, limitless extension (quadruply-extended space-time) constitute the distinguishing hypothesis of that geometry as a theorem-lattice.

To this is added a simplistic notion of imaginary *physical space-time,* which might be fairly described, otherwise, as "Things do rattle about if placed in an otherwise empty bucket." Given, an object, assumed to correspond to an actual or possible sense-perception: According to the hypothesis for simple space-time, a point, whose intrinsic space-time size is absolute zero, can be located as part of that object, and also as a place in quadruply-extended space-time. Extending that notion, any object can be mapped as occupying a relevant region of space-time; this mapping is done in terms of a large density of such points common, as places, to the object, and to space-time.

It is assumed, next, that motion of objects can be tracked in this manner (in quadruply-extended space-time). However, physical experience shows that space-time alone could not determine the motion of objects. The variability in the experienced motion, is assumed to correspond to what we may term *physical attributes,* such as mass, charge, smell, and so on. The notion of

extension can be applied to each of these attributes. This prompts us to think of *physical space-time,* to think in terms of multiply-extended magnitudes in a way which is more general than the intuitive notion of simple space-time.

If it is adopted as part of the hypothesis for the system, that apparent cause-effect relations affecting motion can be adequately expressed in terms of manifold such assumedly physical factors of extension, the result of such attempted constructions of a physical space-time, is describable as an assumed *physical space-time manifold.* That geometry of the naive imagination, is the general map for the empiricist mathematical physics of Paolo Sarpi and such of his followers as Galileo Galilei, Francis Bacon, Thomas Hobbes, René Descartes, Isaac Newton, Leonhard Euler, Lord Rayleigh, and so on.[24]

That simplistic approach to mathematical physics, is the implicit basis for what are, presently, generally accepted notions bearing upon economics, both within the profession, and among illiterates, alike. This mechanistic schema of the Newtonians, is otherwise the pervasive misconception of the term "science" itself. This is the customary referent for use of the cant-phrase "scientific objectivity."

Riemann introduces this consideration in the two opening paragraphs. He attacks the problems of that naive geometry itself, thus:

It is known, that geometry presupposes both the conception of space, and the first principles for constructions in space as something given. It gives only nominal definitions, while the essential determinations appear in the form of axioms. The relation of these presuppositions remains in darkness; one has insight neither, if and how far

---

24. See discussion of Sarpi and his followers, in Lyndon H. LaRouche, Jr., "Why Most Nobel Prize Economists Are Quacks," *EIR* Aug. 4, 1995, *passim.*

their connection is necessary, nor, a priori, if they are possible. From Euclid to Legendre, to name the most famous of recent workers in geometry, this darkness has been lifted neither by the mathematicians, nor by the philosophers who have busied themselves with it. . . . A necessary consequence of this [the foregoing considerations—LHL], *is that the principles of geometry cannot be derived from general notions of magnitude, but rather that those properties, by which space is distinguished from other thinkable threefold extensions of magnitude, can be gathered only from experience.*[25]

Or, as Riemann puts the latter point at the conclusion of the same dissertation, within "the domain of physics," as distinct from mathematics per se.[26]

The first mathematical challenge posed by the mere general idea of a *physical space-time manifold* is embodied in the fact, that such an idea precludes all notions of a static geometry. Since the close of the last century, it has been noted frequently, that once we take into account the fact, that we can not reduce the variability of velocities of motion, among even simple objects, to some principles of bare space-time, the bare notions of space and time must be expelled from mathematical physics.[27] Since our notions of mathematics are derived from the threefold space of our imagination, how shall physics account mathematically for the distortion which the evidence of a physical space-time manifold imposes upon the possibility of representing motion in space-time?

Let us interrupt the description of Riemann's dissertation briefly, to inform the reader that, in the next few paragraphs, we are now about to address, not all of the crucial points of the dissertation, but several which all bear implicitly upon the problems of "economic modelling"; One of these most explicitly.

In addressing the first of a series of implications, on the concept of an n-fold extended magnitude,[28] Riemann states he has found but two existing literary sources which have been of assistance to him: Gauss's second treatise on biquadratic residues,[29] and a philosophical investigation of Johann Friedrich Herbart.[30] Then, in the opening paragraph of the next subsection, on the relations of measure,[31] he states a crucial point on which our attention will be fixed: "Consequently, if we are to gain solid ground, an abstract investigation in formulas is indeed not to be evaded, but the results of that will allow a representation in the garment of geometry. . . . [T]he foundations are contained in Privy Councillor Gauss's treatise on curved surfaces."[32] Let the

---

25. Riemann, *Werke*, pp. 272-273: *Bekanntlich setzt die Geometrie sowohl den Begriff des Raumes, als die ersten Grundbegriffe für die Constructionen im Raume als etwas Gegebenes voraus. Sie giebt von ihnen nur Nominaldefinitionen, während die wesentlichen Bestimmungen in Form von Axiomen auftreten. Das Verhältniss dieser Voraussetzungen bleibt dabei im Dunkeln; man sieht weder ein, ob und wie weit ihre Verbindung nothwendig, noch a priori, ob sie möglich ist. Diese Dunkelheit wurde auch von Euklid bis Legendre, um den berühmtesten neueren Bearbeiter der Geometrie zu nennen, weder von Mathematikern, noch von den Philosophen, welche sich damit beschäftigten, gehoben. . . . Hiervon aber ist eine notwendige Folge, dass die Sätze der Geometrie sich nicht aus allgemeinen Größenbegriffen ableiten lassen, sondern dass diejenigen Eigenschaften, durch welche sich der Raum von anderen denkbaren dreifach ausgedehnten Größen unterscheidet, nur aus der Erfahrung entnommen werden können.*

26. Ibid. p. 286.

27. This issue was already stated, in their own terms, by Leibniz and Jean Bernouilli, in the 1690s. Once Christiaan Huyghens learned, in 1677, that, during the previous year his former student, Ole Rømer, had given a measurement of approximately 3×10^8 meters per second for the "speed of light," Huyghens recognized immediately the implications of a constant rate of retarded light propagation for reflection and refraction. (See Poul Rasmussen, "Ole Rømer and the Discovery of the Speed of Light," *21st Century Science & Technology*, Spring 1993. See also,

Christiaan Huyghens, *Treatise on Light* (1690) (New York: Dover Publications, Inc., 1962).) Leibniz's attacks on the incompetence, for physics, of the algebraic method employed by Newton, and his understanding of the requirement of a "non-algebraic" (i.e., transcendental) method, instead, reflected most significantly the demonstration of principles of reflection and refraction of light consistent with a constant rate of retarded propagation which is independent of the notions possible in terms of a naive physical space-time.

28. Op. cit., "I. Begriff einer *n*fach ausgedehnten Größe," pp. 273-276.

29. *"Zur Theorie der biquadratischen Reste,"* Gauss, *Werke*, Vol. II, E. Schering, ed., pp. 313-385, including notes by Shering.

30. J.F. Herbart was a famous opponent of the philosophy of Immanuel Kant. He came under the influence of Professor of History Friedrich Schiller at the Jena university, and became later a protégé of Wilhelm von Humboldt, assigned to Kant's former university at Königsberg for long period. During the middle of the 1830s, Herbart was invited to C.F. Gauss's Göttingen university, where he delivered a famous series of lectures. It was in this connection that Riemann was first exposed to him. Riemann's critical references to some of Herbart's arguments contain the material referenced at this point in his *Hypothesen*; see *"I. Zur Psychologie unter Metaphysik,"* Werke, pp. 509-520.

31. *"Maßverhältnisse, deren . . . ,"* p. 276.

32. *"Es wird daher, um festen Boden zu gewinnen, zwar eine abstracte Untersuchung in Formeln nicht zu vermeiden sein, die Resultate derselben aber werden sich im geometrischen Gewande darstellen lassen. . . . [S]ind die Grundlagen enthalten in der berühmten Abhandlung des Herrn Geheimen Hofraths Gauss über die krummen Flächen."*

echo of "a representation in the garment of geometry" resonate throughout reflections upon what now follows.

In 1952, when the writer re-read this Riemann dissertation in the light of Cantor's Aleph-transfinites, the writer's own relevant form of "relations of measure," was already the same principle of measurement subsumed by that same general conception of physical-economic "not-entropy" described here. Define the "not-entropy" of a physical-(macro)economic process in the general terms employed above. Consider the following preparatory steps required for broadly defining the meaning of "relations of measure" applicable to such an economic process.

Assign some small, but significant "free energy" ratio, such as the suggested 5% figure. This ratio subsumes the following included inequalities: The potential relative population-density, must rise; the demographic characteristics of family households and of the population as a whole, must improve; the capital-intensity and power-intensity, measured in physical terms, must increase, per capita, per household, and per unit of relevant land-area employed; a portion of the "free energy" margin sufficient to sustain a value constantly not less than 5% free-energy ration, must be reinvested in the productive cycle, to the effects of increasing the capital-intensity, the power-intensity, and the scale of the process. The requirement of the constant 5% growth-factor, serves as a rule-of-thumb standard, to ensure that the margin of growth is sufficient to prevent the process from shifting, as a whole, into an entropic phase.

Those are the effective relations of measure characteristic of successful national economies. Adopting those relations of measure, to what sort of physical space-time are we implicitly referring? Look back to the earlier history of development of modern science; there, one encounters some useful suggestions.

The founding work of modern science, Nicolaus of Cusa's *De docta ignorantia,* introduced the notion in the form of a self-subsisting process, the isoperimetric principle, to supersede the axioms of point and straight line. This isoperimetric principle, in the guise of the cycloid of generalized refraction of light, became associated with the notions of "least action," "least time," and "least constraint." From the referenced work of R@tomer and Huyghens, through Jean Bernoulli and Leibniz, and beyond, the notion of a principle of retarded propagation of light, as associated with the isoperimetric principle, etc., has served as the yardstick, the "clock," of relative value for physical science in general. Now, noting that, define the motion of a not-entropic economic process relative to the measure provided by the "clock."

As measured by that "clock," we measure, in first approximation, the relations of production and consumption in societies taken as integrated entireties. This is a statistical beginning, but not the required standard of measure. These first estimates must be expressed in a second approximation, in terms of *rates of change of the relations of production and consumption*; that, in turn, must be expressed as *rates of increase of potential relative population-density.*

This, in turn, requires that we re-examine the notion of economic not-entropy. The content of the not-entropy is not measured in terms of the increase of the numbers of market-basket objects, and of the ratio of production to consumption. Rather, the validity of efforts to measure performance in those market-basket terms, depends upon the coherence of that estimate with increase of the potential relative population-density. In other words, economic not-entropy, expressed as we have described its statistical approximation above, must parallel increase of the potential relative population-density It is the increase of the potential relative population-density, as such, which is the ontological content of the not-entropy being estimated.

So, instead of measuring distance in physical-economic space-time in centimeter-gram-second, or analogous qualities of units, we measure that not-entropic effect expressed as increase of potential relative population-density. The value of the action is expressed *implicitly* in the latter measure. As we wrote, near the outset here: It is the implicit social content of each valid axiomatic revolutionary discovery in science or art, which defines human knowledge: not Wiener's mechanistic, statistical approach. That implicit social content, is the efficiency of practiced ideas, to the effect of main-

---

p. 276. Riemann is referencing one of the most famous, and influential discoveries by C.F. Gauss, made doubly famous by the problems of Special Relativity. Gauss's summary work on this subject was originally published, in Latin, in 1828, under the title *"Disquisitiones Generales Circa Superficies Curvas,"* Werke, Vol. IV, pp. 217-258. However, it would be useful to read, also, Gauss's *"Theorie der krummen Flächen,"* Vol. VIII, pp. 363-452.

taining and also increasing the rate of increase of society's potential relative population-density.

Consider the implications, for mathematics, of the points we have just summarized.

The first step in constructing a "physical-economic space-time manifold," uses the countable categories of items indicated for such statistical studies. That second step is to employ that data-base to provide a means of measuring relations within the system in terms of the estimated relative not-entropy of the ongoing economic process as an integrated entirety. The third step, is to estimate the rate of not-entropy, as checked with and corrected by a comparison with the rate of not-entropy expressed in terms of potential relative population-density. The third step's results must be reflected, as correction, upon the standards earlier estimated for the second step; that latter correction, must, in turn, be reflected upon the valuation of the statistical categories employed in the first step. Riemann's work provides a conceptual guide for that multifacetted effort.

By introducing the principle, that relations of measure in physical-economic space-time are governed by the principle of rate of increase of potential relative population-density, we have located the mathematical representation of economic processes within non-Euclidean geometry, as Riemann's dissertation defines the notion of such a geometry. To wit: In the graphs which we are able to construct, using appropriate market-basket data, we have embedded our standard of measure.

In Eratosthenes' time, to the eye of the observer, the Earth was flat, and, therefore, it must be measured according to what passed for principles of plane geometry at that time. By showing that method of measurement to lead to a devastating contradiction, if regarded in a certain way, Eratosthenes required what became known later as principles of geodesy to be employed—the principles governing measure in curved surfaces, in place of the standards of plane geometry.

As we noted, above: Later, during the last quarter of Europe's Seventeenth Century, once the astronomical researches of Ole R@tomer had established a definite rate for retarded propagation of light radiation, the combined work of Huyghens, Leibniz, and Jean Bernoulli established the necessity for replacing the naive, Sarpi-Galileo form of perfectly continuous Euclidean space-time by a physical space-time of fivefold extension, a space-time which, according to Leibniz, was not perfectly continuous.[33] In addition to quadruply-extended space and time, the rate of retarded propagation of light must be added as another extension. To reflect that, it was necessary to adopt Cusa's notion that the idea of triply-extended space must be subordinated to what Cusa was first to define, what was later named the transcendental domain, in which the isoperimetric principle, rather than axiomatic points and lines, defines the hypothesis underlying measure.

And, so on, in history since then.

In that tradition, aided by Riemann's work, we are able to present the geometric shadow of the corresponding n-fold physical space-time manifold of physical economy, as an image in a triply-extended domain. Which is as if to say with the twenty-seven-year-old Riemann,[34] that "an abstract investigation in formulas is indeed not to be evaded, but the results of that will allow a representation in the garment of geometry." The essential qualifications are, that we must never forget that that is precisely what we have done.[35]

To understand the relevant contribution by Riemann in the degree required for our purposes here, we must return to read Riemann in the very special way this writer reread Riemann's dissertation back in 1952. We must focus upon the specificity of that deeper insight into Riemann's discovery which had been prompted by this writer's study of Cantor's work.

Density of Discontinuities

If the later *Beiträge*[36] is Georg Cantor's most important formal contribution to mathematics, his most important contribution to the philosophy of mathematics came in writings during the middle 1880s, from the appearance of his 1883 *Grundlagen…*[37] to nearly a decade

---

33. This was the issue of Newton devotee Leonhard Euler's notorious 1761 attack upon Leibniz's *Monadology.* See Lyndon H. LaRouche, Jr., "Appendix XI: Euler's Fallacies on the Subjects of Infinite Divisibility and Leibniz's Monads," *The Science of Christian Economy* (Washington, D.C.: Schiller Institute, 1991), pp. 407-425.

34. Riemann was born on Sept. 17, 1826 (*Werke*, p. 541); the presentation of his habilitation dissertation occurred on June 10, 1854 (ibid., p. 272n).

35. If that fact were not made plain to students, and other "consumers" of economists' work-product, the result would tend to be the type of superstition already typical of most Nobel-Prize-winning economists and their dupes. What we know is that for which we are able to account in terms of the manner in which we came to know it.

36. Op. cit.

37. Georg Cantor, *Grundlagen einer allgemeinen Mannigfaltigkeitslehre* (Leipzig: 1883). Originally published as *Über unendliche lineare*

prior to his 1897 *Beiträge.* . . .[38] This includes a series of communications on the subject of the historical, philosophical, and methodological implications of the notion of the *transfinite.* From the *Grundlagen* onwards, during this interval, Cantor addressed chiefly formal issues of the mathematical transfinite, but, also, if in passing, of the *ontological transfinite.*[39]

Briefly, among the historical-philosophical observations, Cantor identifies his notion of the transfinite to be coincident with Plato's *ontological* notion of *Becoming,* and his notion of the mathematical *Absolute* to be coincident with Plato's *ontological* conception of the *Good.* For the application of this to Riemann's discovery, the relevant issues are summarily implicit in Plato's *Parmenides* dialogue. The case in point is as follows.

In the *Parmenides,* Plato's Socrates lures Parmenides, the leader of the methodologically reductionist Eleatic school, into exposing the inescapable and axiomatically devastating paradoxes of the Eleatic dogma. The paradox is both formal and ontological, most significantly ontological. In the dialogue itself, Plato supplies only an ironical, passing reference to the solution for this paradox: Parmenides has left the principle of *change* out of account. The functional relationship of Plato's implicit argument to Riemann's discovery, is direct; Cantor's references to Plato's *Becoming* and *Good,* are directly relevant to both. Riemann himself supplies a significant clue to these connections, in a posthumously published, anti-Kant document presented under the title *"Zur Psychologie und Metaphysik."*[40]

The relevant aspects of the common connections are essentially the following.

Reference the stated general case of a series of theorem-lattices, considered in a sequence corresponding to increases in potential relative population-density of a culture. We are presented, thus, with a lattice of theorem-lattices, each separated from the other by one or more absolute, logical-axiomatic discontinuities (e.g., mathematical discontinuities). Question: What is the ordering relationship among the members of such a lattice of theorem-lattices? Consider this as potentially an ontological paradox of the form treated by Plato's *Parmenides.*

Some discoveries may occur, in reality, either prior to or after certain other discoveries; however, they must always occur after some discoveries, and prior to some others. This is true for discoveries in the Classical art-forms and related matters, as for natural science. In other words, each valid axiomatic-revolutionary discovery in human knowledge, is identifiable as a term of the lattice of theorem-lattices, it exists only by means of a necessary predecessor, and is itself a necessary predecessor of some other terms. This is the historical reality of the cumulative valid progress in knowledge, to date, of the human species as a whole. This is, for reasons broadly identified above, the function which locates the cause for successive increases in mankind's potential relative population-density. Question: What is the ordering-principle which might subsume all possible terms of this lattice of theorem-lattices?

On the relatively simpler level, if the series of terms being examined is of a certain quality, the solution to the type of paradox offered in the *Parmenides* is foreseeable. If the collection of terms can be expressed as an ordered series, or an ordered lattice, the terms can be expressed as either all, or at least some of the terms generated by a constant ordering principle, a constant concept of difference (change) among the terms. In that case, the single notion of that difference (change) may be substituted for a notion of each of the terms of the collection. In terms of the Plato dialogue, the *Many* can be represented, thus, by a *One.*

Cantor's principal work is centered upon the case of the representation of the Many of an indefinitely extended mathematical series, by a One. The treatment of the notion of mathematical *cardinality* in this scheme of reference, leads toward the notion of the higher transfinite, the Alephs, and to the generalization of the notion of counting in terms of cardinalities as such. The latter corresponds, most visibly, to the idea of the density of formal discontinuities represented by compared accumulations of valid axiomatic-revolutionary discoveries. Question: How is the latter Many to be represented by a constructible, or otherwise cognizable One?

The notion associated with the solution to that challenge is already to be found in the work of Plato: the

---

Punktmannigfaltigkeiten, Werke pp. 139-246.

38. See Note 4, above.

39. E.g., *Mitteilungen zur Lehre vom Transfiniten, Werke,* pp. 378-440.

40. *Werke,* pp. 509-520. My colleague, Dr. Jonathan Tennenbaum, has pointed out C.F. Gauss's devastating ridicule of Kant's work. Cantor, in the *Mitteilungen,* expresses similar contempt for Kant.

notion of *higher hypothesis.* However, using the terms from Riemann's dissertation, the conceptualization of this solution, actual knowledge of this notion of *higher hypothesis,* as an ontological actuality, "will be gathered only from experience."

Consider the case of the student who has been afforded that Classical-humanist form of education, in which reliving the act of original axiomatic-revolutionary discoveries of principle, is the only accepted standard for knowledge. That student has the repeated experience of applying a principle of discovery which leads consistently to valid axiomatic-revolutionary discoveries. That repeated experience, that reconstructed mental act of discovery, has been rendered an object—an *idea*—accessible to conscious reflection, an object of thought. Like any such object of thought, that state of mind can be recalled, and also deployed. How should we name this quality—this *type*[41]—of thought-object?

Just as Plato identifies a valid new set of interdependent axioms, underlying a corresponding theorem-lattice, as an *hypothesis,* so he references the type of thought-object to which we have just made reference as an *higher hypothesis.* The fact that the mode of effecting valid axiomatic-revolutionary hypotheses may be itself improved, signifies a possible series of transitions to successively superior (more powerfully efficient) qualities of *higher hypothesis,* a state of mental activity which Plato's method recognizes as *hypothesizing the higher hypothesis.* The latter is congruent with Cantor's general notion of the transfinite; in other words, Plato's ontological state of *Becoming.*[42]

In the posthumously published paper, *"Zur Pyschologie und Metaphysik,"* Riemann identifies both "hypothesis" and "higher hypotheses" as of a species he names *Geistesmassen.* This term is synonymous with Leibniz's use of "Monad," and the present writer's preference for the term "thought-object": ideas which correspond to the types of formal discontinuities being considered here. Every person who has reexperienced, repeatedly, valid axiomatic-revolutionary discoveries in the Classical-humanist manner referenced, is familiar with the existence of such ideas.

Now, that said, back to Plato's *Parmenides.* Consider the case, that the principle of change, the One, ordering the generation of the members of the collection, the Many, is of the form of higher hypothesis. This is the case, if the members of the collection termed the Many, each represent valid axiomatic-revolutionary discoveries. Contrary to Kant's *Critiques,*[43] the principle of valid axiomatic-revolutionary discovery is cognizable, and that from the vantage-point already identified here.

Also, contrary to Kant's notorious *Critique of Judgment,* the same principle governs Classical forms of artistic creativity: as in the history of the pre-development of the method of motivic (modal) thorough-composition. The discoveries associated with this form of creativity are exemplified by Mozart (1782-86) and by Beethoven's revolution in motivic thorough-composition, as exemplified by the late string quartets.[44] Johannes Brahms is also a master of that method of coherent musical creativity.

The immediately foregoing several summary observations serve to indicate the accessibility of the notion of a comprehensible ordering of a lattice of theorem-lattices. Relative to the economic-theoretical implications of Riemann's dissertation, the point to be added here, is that this notion is not only intrinsically cognizable: This is a physically efficient notion, and is ontological in that sense. It is also ontological in a sense supplied earlier by Heracleitus and Plato.

The question is at least as old as these two ancient Greeks.

Once the ontological issue of Plato's *Parmenides* is taken into consideration, the following question is implicitly posed. The subsuming One is a *perfect* expression for the domain typified by the subsumed Many. Consequently, does the ontologically intrinsic, relative *imperfection* of that Many signify that the ontological actuality reposes in the One, rather than the particular phenomena, or ideas of the Many? The One always has the content of *change,* relative to the particularity of each among the Many. Does this imply that that *change*

---

41. Using the term "type" in Cantor's sense.

42. It is not necessary to treat the subject of the *Good* in the present context. On that see Lyndon H. LaRouche, Jr., "The Truth About Temporal Eternity," *Fidelio,* Summer 1994, *passim.*

43. *Critique of Pure Reason* (1781), *Prolegomena to a Future Metaphysic* (1783), *Critique of Practical Reason* (1788), and *Critique of Judgment* (1790).

44. See Lyndon H. LaRouche, Jr., "Mozart's 1782-1786 Revolution in Music," *Fidelio,* Winter 1992, and Bruce Director, "What Mathematics Can Learn From Classical Music," *Fidelio,* Winter 1994. The late Beethoven string quartets referenced are: E-flat major, Opus 127; B-flat major (The "Grosse Fuge" quartet), Opus 130; A-minor, Opus 132; B-flat major ("Grosse Fuge"), Opus 133; and, F major, Opus 135.

Felix Klein (left) and Leonhard Euler. Klein attempted to defend Euler's scurrilous attack on Gottfried Leibniz in the matter of the "infinite series," perpetrating a monstrous fraud.

is ontologically primary, relative to the content of each and all of the Many? In other words, is this *ontological* significance of Heracleitus' "nothing is constant but change" to be applied?

That is the type of significance which the term "ontologically transfinite" has, when applied to the formally or geometrically transfinite orderings presented, respectively, by Cantor and Riemann's dissertation.

Put the same proposition in the context of physical-economic processes.

Let the term "lattice of theorem-lattices" identify an array of theorem-lattices generated by a constant principle of axiomatic-revolutionary discovery: an higher hypothesis. Then, that higher hypothesis is the One which subsumes the Many theorem-lattices. Relative to any and all such theorem-lattices, it is that higher hypothesis which is, apparently, the efficient cause of the not-entropy generated in practice. It is that higher hypothesis which is (again: apparently) the relatively primary, efficient cause of the not-entropy. It is that higher hypothesis, which is, relatively primary, ontologically.

As Leonhard Euler, and, later Felix Klein,[45] refused

to take into consideration: Correlation, even astonishingly precise correlation, is not necessarily cause. The cause is not the *formal* not-entropy of such a lattice of theorem-lattices; *the cause is expressed in those hermetically sovereign, creative powers of each individual person's mental processes: the developable potential for generating, receiving, replicating, and practicing efficiently the axiomatic-revolutionary discoveries in science and Classical art-forms.* This notion of causation, drawn from "experience," is the crux of the determination of a Riemannian physical-economic space-time.

Mankind's success in generating, successfully, upward-reaching phase-shifts in potential relative population-density, demonstrates that the universe is so composed, that the *developable* creative-mental potential of the individual human mind is capable of mastering that universe with increasing efficiency. On this account, the very idea of "scientific objectivity" is a fraud, particularly if expressed as an empiricist, or "materialist" notion. *All knowledge is essentially subjective; all proof is, in the last analysis, essentially subjective.* It is our critical examination of those processes of the individual mind, through which valid axiomatic-revolutionary discoveries are generated, or their original generation replicated, which is the source of knowledge. This is shown to represent a valid claim to knowledge, at least relatively so, by the success of axiomatic-revolutionary scientific and artistic progress, in increasing mankind's potential relative population-density. It is through the critical self-examination of the individual mental processes through which such discoveries are generated, and their generation replicated, that true scientific knowledge is attained: the

---

45. Felix Klein, *Famous Problems of Elementary Geometry* (1895), W.W. Beman and D.E. Smith, trans., R.C. Archibald, ed. (New York: Chelsea Publishing Co., 1980), pp. 49-80. Klein is probably aware that the proof that **pi** is transcendental, was first given, from the standpoint of geometry, by Nicolaus of Cusa; he knows, without question, that the transcendental character of **pi** was conclusively established by Leibniz et al., during the 1690s. Yet, he insists that the transcendence of *pi* was first proven by F. Lindemann, in 1882! The reason for Klein's gentle fraud, is that he is defending Euler's attack on Leibniz in the matter of "infinite series." Thus, Klein is motivated by his insistence upon an Euler-based algebraic "proof" (and, no other!) even at the expense of perpetrating a monstrous fraud on the history of science.

which, therefore, might be better termed "scientific subjectivity."

Notably, valid axiomatic-revolutionary discoveries can not be "communicated" explicitly. Rather, they are caused to reappear in other minds only by inducing the other person to replicate the process of the original act of discovery. One may search the medium of communication for eternity, and never find a trace of the original communication of such an idea to any person. What is communicated is the catalyst which may prompt the hearer to activate the appropriate generative processes within his or her own fully autonomous creative-mental processes. The result may thus appear, to the "information theorist," to be the greatest secret code in the universe: In effect, by this means, the means of a Classical-humanist mode of education, vastly more "information" is transmitted than the band-pass is capable of conducting.

Thus, the following:

1) The cause of the not-entropic characteristic of healthy physical-economy, is the exercise of the developable and sovereign mental-creative potential of the individual human mind. It is the input to that potential, which produces the efficient not-entropy as an output.

2) The crucial social part of the process is the correlated form of individual potential for being stimulated to replicate the relevant act of discovery.

3) The human precondition, is the development of the individuals and their relations within society to foster this generation and replication of such ideas.

4) The efficient practice of this social process depends upon the preparation of man-altered nature to become suitable for the successful (not-entropic) application of these discoveries to nature. Those are the axioms governing that causation essential to the geometry of physical-economic processes. The not-entropic image of an implied cardinality function in terms of densities of singularities per chosen interval of relevant action, is the reflection of those axioms and their implications. The set of constraints (e.g., inequalities), governing acceptable changes in relations of production and consumption, must therefore be in conformity with such a notion of a not-entropic cardinality function: that set of inequalities must be characteristically not-entropic in effect.

As was noted near the outset here: *A mathematical solution (in the formal sense) would be desirable, but a conceptual view was indispensable.* The most important thing, is to know what to do. Above all, we must be guided by these considerations in defining the policies of education and popular culture which we foster and employ for the development of the mental-creative potential of the individual in society, especially the young.

Epilogue: the Interaction Principle

Respecting the interaction of the two, axiomatically inconsistent systems: the characteristically entropic, linear monetary-financial process and the characteristically not-entropic physical-economic process.

There are three typical states to be considered: 1) The two processes, the monetary-financial parasite and the physical-economic process, are "symbiotically" inter-linked, with the parasite dominant, but with such constraints that a phase-shift of the economic process into an entropic mode does not occur; 2) The two processes are similarly linked, but the dominating monetary-financial process progressively de-couples itself from the economic process; 3) The physical-economic process is employed by government to regulate the monetary and financial process to such a degree, that the latter becomes a subsidiary institution of the former. The first, was what might be termed the "normal" state of symbiosis within the industrialized economies, during the several centuries preceding 1963. The second, is the presently, hyperbolically degenerating state of the combined world economy and monetary-financial systems. The third, is the preferred arrangement, implicitly defined by the George Washington administration of the U.S. Federal republic: the so-called "model" represented by the Franklin-Hamilton-Carey-List "American System of political-economy."[46]

The crucial issue of the interaction, is the role of the sovereign nation-state form of national economy. "Experience," in Riemann's referenced sense of *Erfahrung,* informs us that the achievement of the most desirable, third form of interaction requires a strong role of a sovereign nation-state's government in the economy. The U.S.A.'s historical experience clearly indicates what the outlines of those governmental functions, on several levels, must be.

The national government must retain sovereign responsibility for regulation of the currency and national

---

46. See, for example, *The Political Economy of the American Revolution,* Nancy Spannaus and Christopher White, eds. (New York: Campaigner Publications, 1977).

credit, monetary, and financial affairs generally, and conditions of trade. This sovereign authority must be applied most emphatically to international affairs, and, as may be deemed necessary for national economic security, in some limited aspects of domestic commerce. Government, at the various national, regional,[47] and local levels, must assume responsibility for providing essential basic economic infrastructure, including measures to ensure adequate quality of universal education, health-care delivery, and promotion of scientific and technological progress.[48]

It is desirable that the preponderance of remaining economic activity be accomplished through privately owned farms and other enterprises. The economic principle governing this is encountered as early as the Fifteenth-Century France of Louis XI, and, more generally, in the nation-states of western Europe. Exemplary of those origins of the modern private enterprise, is the use of governmental patents to grant limited-term monopolies on manufacture and sale to inventors and their business associates; this is the origin of the limited-term, modern patent issued to inventors. The social function of private ownership, is to foster the application of the creative powers and intellectual prudence and courage of the individual entrepreneur, as a person, to the fostering of the generation and efficient use of improvements in methods and practices to the economic advantage of the nation and humanity more generally.

The division of authority and responsibility between the state and the private entrepreneur, is defined essentially by the nature of the social responsibilities implicitly assumed, or neglected by each. The development of basic economic infrastructure, represents the requirement, that a responsibility be met to the entire land-area of the relevant political unit, to the population considered as a whole, and to those general matters in which only government can assume efficient direct responsibility. Within the framework of governmental responsibility to provide or to regulate, the private entrepreneur should enjoy a broad, if nonetheless delimited authority.

That is not, as some misguided ideologues would describe it, a "mixed economy"; it is the only sane construction of a modern economy.

The most efficient performance of national economies has been achieved through what President Charles de Gaulle's France knew as "indicative planning." The state employs its combined monopolies of regulation and scale of economic operations, to foster the rate of investment and growth in those projects and other special categories of enterprise, which will supply the relatively greatest rate of well-balanced growth of the economy as a whole. The use of national credit, to foster beneficial and needed public works, and large-scale science-driver programs, such as aerospace development ventures, are typical of the strategic uses of concentrating public credit to foster the relatively highest rates of long-term growth and development in the economy as a whole.

A monopoly on the creation of public credit, as provided by Article I of the U.S. Federal Constitution, and the focussing of that public credit to foster full employment in combined public and private enterprises most beneficial to the general interest in sustained technological progress, is the principal instrument through which the government fosters optimal rates of growth of income, output, and tax-revenue base, in the economy as a whole.

The general rule which ought to be applied, is that, in the physical economy as such, the state must foster relatively high rates of capital-intensity, power-intensity, and scientific and technological progress. This is achieved chiefly, by the use of tax-incentives and deployment of low-cost public credit, to favor the recycling of margins of relative "free energy" in economic output into technology-driver forms of productive and related investment.

In short, the problem of the interaction between the two axiomatically distinct kinds of processes, is almost entirely a matter of the responsibility, by governments of sovereign national economies, to regulate monetary and financial affairs. The object of such regulation must be to bring about and maintain the third of the three possible forms of interaction identified here.

---

47. In the U.S.A.'s Federal constitutional tradition, the regional authority lies primarily with the Federal state, except as national interest may prescribe a Federal responsibility.

48. National water-management, including principal ports and inland waterways, watersheds, and relevant sanitation are included. Also, general public transportation should be either a governmental economic responsibility, or government-regulated area of private investment. The organization and regulation of adequate national power-supplies, adequately provided for the regions and localities, is a key governmental responsibility. Basic urban infrastructure is also a governmental responsibility, chiefly of local government under national guidance and state regulation as to standards.